Blue Valley

An Ecological Memoir

By Luanne Armstrong

Maa Press, Nelson, B.C.

Copyright 2007 by Luanne Armstrong

ALL RIGHTS RESERVED. No part of this book may be reproduced or transmitted in any form or by any means whatsoever without written permission from the publisher except by a reviewer, who may quote brief passages in a review. For information, write Maa Press.

Cover image by Dorothy Woodend
Book design by Angela Lockerbie

Printed in Canada by Hignell Book Printing on 100% post-consumer use, recycled paper.

Published in Canada by:
Maa Press
1-4925 Marello Road,
Nelson, British Columbia
Sinixt Territory
V1L 6X4, Canada
maapress@netidea.com
www.maapress.ca

Library and Archives Canada Cataloguing in Publication

Armstrong, Luanne, 1949-
    Blue valley : an ecological memoir / Luanne Armstrong.

(Colours of the Columbia series Blue book)
ISBN 978-0-9685302-4-5

    1. Armstrong, Luanne, 1949-. 2. Columbia Mountains Region (B.C.)--Biography. 3. Authors, Canadian (English)--20th century--Biography. I. Title. II. Series.

PS8551.R7638Z464 2007   C813'.54   C2007-903723-2

Blue Valley

An Ecological Memoir

Thank you

Many people were of support and assistance as I was writing this book. At UBC, Dr. Carl Leggo, Dr. Lynn Fels and George McWhirter gave valuable support and advice. In addition, many people have helped in other ways; above all, my children: Avril Woodend, Dorothy Woodend, Nat Morris and Geronimo Morris, and my family, in particular my brothers, Philip Armstrong and Bill Armstrong. The Women Writing Women group provided valuable feedback and advice. Dr. Clair Woodbury and Mary Woodbury provided a writing haven along with support and advice and Evelyn and George Armstrong welcomed me to another writing haven, my 'other home' on Nicola Lake.

Many others, including Jane Hamilton, Jean Rystaad, Zoe Landale, Dorothy Woodend and Sheila Peters, were all both excellent readers and critics. Thanks to Peter Duryea for his wonderful work in organizing the Sense of Place workshop at Tipi Camp on Kootenay Lake.

I owe a very special debt to K. Linda Kivi, for conversation about shared ideas and concerns and for her support in the publication of this work and for her fine and perceptive editing. And a special thanks to Nadene Morton, with whom I began my writing journey at UVic in 1979.

And of course there were many others who have helped in so many small but important ways that I can't name them all but I do deeply appreciate them.

Dedication

This work is dedicated to two special people whose love and care has sustained my life: my friend and neighbour, Alan James Wilson, whose life was cut short by cancer in 2002, and my mother, Dorothy Anne Klingensmith Armstrong.

Preface

IT'S A LATE AFTERNOON in August when my border collie, Kin, and I set out for a walk. Beside the road, fireweed and tansy blaze chartreuse and gold in the tangled brown brush of late summer. This end of August, the farm dozes under a grey sky. A week ago it poured rain for three days, but now it's dry again. Ripe peaches drag the boughs of the peach trees to the ground.

The new summer people, just to the north of the farm, have left for the rest of the summer so I can walk through that part of the lakeshore again. Our beach is a lot quieter without their boat. They spent over an hour one day in their powerboat circling around just off our beach pulling kids behind them on a tube. I know this is fun—I did try it once—but the noise was wearing and after a while I got fed up and waved to indicate that they could please, please go out into the middle of the lake or perhaps to perdition, I really didn't care.

I haven't met them yet. I'm sure they are lovely people. But there is a time-honoured tradition at the farm that we don't mix much with summer people. They're not real neighbours, after all.

But if I get a chance, I'd like to tell these people that where they have recently plunked their cabins, their RVs, their kid's swing set, their tubes and boats and folding plastic chairs and barbecues, the place where they have cleared and graveled roads and dug waterlines, we have always called Sawdust Bay.

Once, about seventy years ago, there was a cabin there, in below the highway, where Mabel and Dick O'Neil and all their kids lived. Pierre Longueval, the man who first homesteaded what became our farm had his sawmill on a granite ledge beside the lake. The old cedar picket fence (that I see now someone has knocked down and driven over), is the remains of the original fence that Pierre built; the pile of sawdust on which the summer people have placed a trailer is where Pete had his original gas sawmill; he cut the lumber for the eighty-year old farmhouse in which I am now living.

Or maybe—but I'm not sure how they would hear it—I could tell these unknown people about the coyote den on the hill just above their cabins. One day, just a few years ago, I was walking there with the dogs, and the coyote bitch came out of the hole she had dug under a rock. She talked to us in an odd voice, a combination of barking and yipping. I had three big male dogs with me and they put their heads down and slunk away as if they had been smacked. I knew the dogs and the coyotes knew each other. Late on winter moonlit nights, I had seen them play along the pasture edge; the coyotes would come out of the trees, the dogs would rush and chase them back, disappearing into that black edge only to come charging back out again, while the coyotes stayed within the tree line and yipped at them.

I had never seen three dogs look so abashed and I wondered what the coyote had said. All I could say was "Sorry, sorry." I backed away as politely as I could and went another way.

Sometimes going for a walk is a very long journey.

What I am doing today is what I have been doing most of my life, walking this land, only now I walk through fifty years of my own history. This land is layered with memories and changes and things that have grown or died and left their remains somewhere here. How many dogs have we buried on this land? And horses. How many generations of cows and pigs and chickens have grown and died and been eaten? Trees have grown and fruited and died or been cut down; roads, paths, trails have been worn into the ground or dug up. There's an apocryphal saying about how, when an elderly person dies, a library burns. I feel a bit like a library some days, my shelves sagging with sepia manuscripts of long ago tales.

Like many families, especially rural families, mine tells stories. Our stories are bound up with four generations who have now lived in this place. We re-live our history in stories that we tell over and over, with variations each time. We never get tired of them. And over time, each version becomes, if not exactly true to the facts, more true to the story. They are tuned and refined. Each time an old story is re-told there are new additions and arguments over whose version is right. Each telling sparks the next story, until the room is a conflagration, an exploding cacophony of rising voices and laughter, which drifts and mingles like smoke and carries us out the door and back to work or chores or whatever other need is calling.

I love to walk and, often, when I walk at the farm, or up the steep mountain slopes above the farm, I start thinking about some of my own questions about what living here means. Walking, for me, is a way of thinking. And today, as always, I am walking through layers of time. There are so many kinds of time here. There is present time, the life I live now, split between the city and here. There is a lifetime of memories of myself growing up here, then my kids growing up here, and then there is the comforting sense of eternity or near eternity, that I can step into whenever I am here in the mountains. One of the reasons I like mountains is they are so present, so huge and so enduring. It's hard to change a mountain. Hard to build on a mountain, hard work to log it, to climb it, to do much of anything to it, although now apparently in Appalachia, they have figured out how to level mountains to get at the coal underneath them.

Mountains are full of secrets and surprises. People come to them for as many reasons as there are people; mountains make both walls and shelters—it's very hard to live here and not feel the rest of the world receding into dim blue distance, to not be reminded that there is another sense of time besides our speedy human perspective. I love mountains because I can hide in them, because they make me feel small and unimportant, and they make the rest of the world go away.

But today I walk past the new neighbours' new-lumber smelling cabins and on up the hill, past the abandoned house that we still call Shelackie's cabin. We first lived there when our parents moved to my grandfather's farm. Then the cabin was bought by the Blackburns, then Beincourts, now it belongs to someone I don't know. Wild roses and buckbrush have sprung up around the front door. I pause at the old workshop; the door sags open and the interior reeks of packrat. Kin snuffles at the walls and digs half-heartedly at the piles of junk.

I head past the workshop, the back way, under the power line. Past Haley's cabins. I like to check on Haley's cabins now and again–no one seems to know who Haley was or why he made these four log cabins–the only story I know is that about a hundred years ago, he trailed a herd of goats over the Purcell mountains to this place. There are still remnants of rock walls and strings of rusty barbed wire where he built an enclosure for his goats. The cabins are almost invisible, crumbling back into soil under a canopy of brush and small trees. One huge Grand Fir has survived fires and clearing and goats. Perhaps it was big enough that Haley left it to grow over his cabin. The fir trees around it are scrawny and haven't grown much over the years–what has grown are the maples and alders, so that the cabins are almost invisible.

Below the cabins is a flattened place in the trees we always called

Preface

Haley's meadow, a place I go once a year for the sweetest of wild blackberries. The blackberry vine has been struggling along for years, almost dead but never quite, covered with grass, under the shade of the alders.

Finally, I walk home again along the highway, past the granite cliffs, the places where the highway department has blasted away at the mountainside to straighten out the curves made by the early road builders, past the corner piece of land on which someone years ago built a plastic and aluminum sided house then stuck a for sale sign on it and disappeared. No one has been here for a long time.

Dogs get old too fast; Kin is panting behind me on the way home instead of scaring me by charging across the road and up the hill and back again, dodging car loads of tourists with screeching brakes and impatient fright on their faces.

Finally we step off the highway back onto the farm, into the yard, under the Transparent apple tree, past the house. Kin lopes ahead of me to take a drink from the bucket by the back door. But I stop. I notice, as I have noticed before, the feeling of being transformed by being home, being private, being safe. A little greedy animal voice inside me chants "mine, ours" and another self that has been walking through the blue shadowed glory of eternity and mountains and outside of present time says "liar, liar" but I have no quarrel with either of them and go on my way, under the enormous walnut tree.

My brother and father lopped the top off it a few years ago but it has now grown a new top and is busy drying the grass and very slowly and steadily killing the sixty-year old Queen Anne cherry tree.

My life here has always been strung on two parallel lines, like the wires my father strung to hold up the long lines of raspberry bushes. There is the land itself, working and living on it, and then there are stories about it. Plus there are the fantasylands I created here as a child.

Walking here now, I walk through stories that dwell in me as I am made from them. Human beings are created by the stories they tell. As soon as we learn to speak, we start to tell stories and as soon as we start to tell stories, we live in the identity those stories make for us. My stories live in me and in this land. They tie me, body and soul, to this place.

Richard Flanagan, the Tasmanian writer, has said that the movement of writers in the last century was away from home but that the movement of writers in this century will be towards home, towards understanding the meaning of home and place. I hope he's right. I believe such understanding is the key to learning to live a genuine and caring sustainable lifestyle. In North America, we have been trying for quite a while to understand our relationship to land, to place, to our slow and hesitant sense of the possibility of becoming indigenous. We have almost no language for this; we left our stories of understanding and belonging back in the places we came from.

Some writers have looked to First Nations for stories of such understanding; other writers have looked back to Europe or to other mythologies for a language of belonging. But our knowledge of where we are and how we live here is still sketchy and still dominated by the idea that this land is a resource, a source of money, more than a place where we now live and are at home.

In the past thirty years Canadian life has undergone a quiet upheaval as people have drifted into cities; the countryside has emptied, changed; farmers, smallholders and loggers have been replaced by retired suburbanites, middle class people seeking peace and quiet, or families that work in town but live just outside of an urban centre. And there are other people, people seeking in some way an alternative to the mainstream direction of North American life.

In the past thirty years, as well, the social, cultural, political and economic life of North America has been in a state of almost continuous change; there were the apocryphal sixties, the anti-war movement, desegregation in the US, the discovery in the early seventies that the environment was fast going to hell, the women's movement which soon morphed into women being involved in all kinds various left wing movements, the peace movement, the new age movement and, of course, on the right, were various reactions to all this change: people heading back to various evangelical and fundamentalist religions, people finding ways to hold the fort, as it were, against the upheaval. And underneath it all, like a slow river of mud, globalization and the free market economy and the forces of economic growth changing peasant and rural economies the world over, with people flooding into giant cities in Brazil and Bangladesh and India and Indonesia as a centuries old way of life was disrupted by the forces of the green revolution coupled with the free market economy.

Although I have watched and read and participated in many of these movements, underneath it all, I always have a peculiar and particular perspective; in a society full of shifting and changing, where the idea of home is often nebulous, where new immigrants to North America struggle to fit in and decide what of their cultural life to keep and what to abandon, I have always been one of the few people I know who was born, grew up and went on living in the same place with the same people and who never wanted to move. Not only that, but I was always, from the day I was old enough to become aware of it, in love with this place and completely at home here, to the exclusion of all others to such an extent that it has never been possible for me to consider any other place my home.

And try as I might to explain this love, I have mostly been met with puzzled looks. One friend said, "It sounds like an addiction," and another friend said, "It sounds like being part of a cult." It has taken me a while to find other writers who echo my own longing for home, other writers whose voices and concepts echo what I know.

As we in North America struggle to make important decisions on land use, clarifying and understanding personal, social, political and economic approaches to land becomes increasingly urgent and I believe, almost terrifyingly important.

The American writer David Duncan has asked, "Is ecological restoration possible without a simultaneous restoration of language? A literature of stories, poems and essays that truly embody the distinctiveness of a particular place and draw their subject matter from the local wellspring of human and more than human lives can be a healing force in an increasingly globalized and technological world."

I believe we need to keep trying to write an authentic literature of place. We need stories that explain a sense of place, of home, knowledge of place, and a story that is equally accessible and culturally coherent. It seems to be generally assumed that narratives about land (even the terms are difficult to articulate) are the place of environmentalists, people with technical expertise about some aspect of natural history or people with a political investment in some aspect of their location. But what then happens to the stories, the knowledge and the understanding that genuinely connect people to a sense of place?

Can we begin to create what biologist Gary Paul Nabhan terms "cultures of habitat," human communities that have a "long history of interaction with one particular kind of terrain and its non-human inhabitants." Other biologists and natural history writers have also considered what it will take to make people of non-aboriginal descent in some sense native to North America. Are there are already pockets of indigenous knowledge, love and understanding within the competing narratives about land and place whose stories we have yet to hear?

I once heard an anthropologist at a Deep Ecology conference describe indigenous communities; she said they share a sense of belonging to the world around them, a sense that they belong to it, not it to them, and therefore a sense of connection that is sustaining and necessary for their whole being, a shared understanding of this interconnection, so that it is something acknowledged, public, social and communally understood; and that in partnership with this goes a tremendous knowledge of the ecosystems around them, knowledge gained through experience and history and familiarity and passed on through stories.

Montana writer William Kittredge says, "We live in stories. What we are is stories. Without storytelling, it's hard to recognize ultimate reasons why one action is more essential than another."

But Kittredge also talks about the political aspect of stories; he says that, "stories which do not change with a changing world" can lead to a "great wreck." To some extent, he believes this is what has already happened as a result of our mythologies, our clashing cultural beliefs about land.

I am also concerned with naming the meaning of a particular place in my own life and by extension in the lives of others. Furthermore, I am the holder and repository, the listener and the reporter for other's stories—my family, my friends and my neighbours—about the same place.

Arguments about the meaning of words like nature and wilderness and wildness seem to be to be potentially endless. Words denote both concepts and the infinitely complex systems of energy behind the concepts.

Stories avoid this problem by inviting us to look into the mirrors of our own selves and form our own complex and mostly unnamed value system out of responses to what we experience.

Of course all stories contain an element of coercion, just as all stories contain an element of education and all stories contain elements of politics—why am I telling you this if not to show you, teach you something, and why are you listening if not to learn?

But stories about the 'natural' world often tend to have a stronger element of coercion than others; nature writers often seem to have, as

Gary Nabhan has written, a limited set of responses, either "reverence, awe, piety, mystical oneness" or doom and gloom 'victim' stories.

To love a place deeply is difficult to write about. All my life I have tested any new experience against the knowledge of my home and what it taught me. I feel I only truly know something when I know it in relationship to my home.

What I know about my home comes not only from living there, but deeply experiencing 'there'—no other place is quite as real to me. I am helpless in this love in the same sense that I am helpless in my love for my children and grandchildren. It is not a choice or something easily subject to analysis and yet it also demands analysis, because it is a relationship, a relationship that is vital to my well-being.

While I write this, I sit at my desk, looking out. This beloved, known world spreads out around me, infinite with possibility. I make patterns from where I sit, looking outside; there is new snow on Castle Mountain and the yellow leaves of the vine maple are still hanging on. Twenty years ago, there were golden larch trees, but my father cut them down and maples and alders have grown to replace them. The Western red cedars have always been there. Beyond them, I can just see the tops of the peach trees that bear cascades of pink and yellow fruit every summer.

I make patterns out of all this while this world makes patterns in me. I want to write my passion for this place, for this world, not as a possessor but as a partner. When I write it down, the words pass through me, the wave leaving the leaf unturned, unmoved in the water. But I make something new, a new pattern, some words and a shape for them.

"Eating peaches is erotic," I once said to someone and she laughed, thinking juicy, succulent, sensual, but we missed each other. I was talking about a circuit sustained, a connection made, a reaching out from the peach tree to me and back again, both of us embracing our purpose: the tree's to make peaches, and mine to eat them. Such a miscommunication is a result of language and culturally embedded meanings. The ecological literacy movement is pitted against a much larger and more entrenched system of capitalistic resource exploitation and an equally intense set of stories about the benefits of commodification and consumerism. Whether we will avoid an ecological wreck in our future is completely unknown. What we do know is that this struggle is deeply embedded in an ongoing social discussion about the meaning and nature of the society in which all of us might want to live, about the ability of stories to give a voice to the voiceless and about the values that ultimately our stories about ourselves and the places we live will transmit to our children.

Telling such stories is a hopeful act, a stone thrown into the dark water of the future. It is an act predicated on the belief that such a story is worth telling and contains a structured meaning that can be transmitted across the gap between writer and reader, between generations, within extended periods of historical time.

Our stories are shaped by and influenced by and are an integral part of whatever landscape within which a story happens—the meaning and interpretation of the place within a story is created by each person within his or her life—each person brings his or her particular understanding to this process. The sense of place is no more neutral in a story than other elements—but is also more indicative of cultural, social, historical, racial, and educated stances re the location of humans in relationship to nature and within land.

One reason environmental issues are so complex is that everyone's story about land and place is so particular, so varied and so personal. Such stories are influenced by a person's biography, their personal narrative, their family history, community history and their sense of location and/or dislocation. Generalizing or making broad statements about a sense of home or the meaning of place invariably leaves someone's experience out. In such circumstances, people over and over again revert to the one place where there is a sure grounding of their experience, in the personal, in relational experiences with nature.

After fifty years of living in the same place, a place that holds my whole life the way a glass bowl holds water, each corner of the road, each tree and bush and mountaintop has a story to tell me, a story I experienced there, that I now re/member there. And I am made by these stories, as much as these stories are mine to make, or mine to tell.

This part of the earth's surface I know intimately; the place is so overgrown and weedy and matted with my story and the story of my family that I sometimes marvel that I can see it at all. I could have been born anywhere, I could have felt the same about anyplace, but this is where I was blown to on a cosmic wind, given to this place and with the great good fortune and presence of mind to fall in love with it as well as to wonder what that means.

Chapter One

THE ROCK SPIRALED towards my head, growing larger and larger while I stood still, too astonished to duck—then the rock hit me and shattered my faith in making friends. Wailing, I ran back inside to my mother.

It was early spring, grey and cold. "Go outside," my mother had snapped. "Go find someone to play with."

I had put on my pink coat and went outside into the dirt road, full of potholes and puddles. I was four. Every day, my mother coaxed my blond curls into ringlets. I wanted more than anything else to do just what my mother said and make friends. I saw a boy in the street, slouching along in a torn jacket and I began to sidle towards him. Perhaps he was who my mother meant. But then he stooped, picked up a rock and threw it, hard.

We had just moved to Riondel, a mining camp in the middle part of the east shore of Kootenay Lake. Before Riondel, we had lived on an isolated farm where we had only one set of neighbours, the Wilsons, who lived a mile down the dirt road. I played sometimes with their son Alan, who was three months younger than me. Alan was blond and frail and I was blonde and tough. We made a good team.

But when we moved to Riondel, my mother promised me, there would be lots of children to play with. I was then three, my older brother, Phillip, was six and just starting school, my younger brother, Bill was only a year old and my mother was pregnant again. The idea of other children was exciting.

When we first moved to Riondel, we lived in a ramshackle two-story company bunkhouse on the outside of town, but the next spring we moved to the unfinished basement of the new house our father was building for us. The basement was damp, the walls and floor were concrete, the only heat was a wood cook stove. This house was in the middle of a lot of other half-finished houses. Outside the basement door was a dirt yard and, beyond that, an expanse of mud that my father had enclosed in a picket fence that he said would be our garden.

Riondel was a straggly kind of place mostly made up of people who had migrated to Canada after World War Two, referred to then, by everyone, simply as DP's, meaning displaced people, immigrants from Europe who had been displaced by the war. Most of them didn't speak English and they lived in a haphazard collection of shacks, tents and bunkhouses built by the Consolidated Mining and Smelting Company, called CM&S or—more simply—the Company. Riondel was at the end of six miles of rutted twisty dirt road that led north from the main highway. Besides the mostly ramshackle collection of dwellings and the muddy dirt roads, there was a gaping hole in the rocks beside the lake that was simply called "the mine." Everyday my father disappeared into that hole and then came home again at night, dirty and tired, carrying his black lunch bucket.

My mother found out who the boy with the rock was and told me to stay away from him. Gradually, my older brother and I began to find the other children and occasionally we played with them. But

Chapter One

more often, we fought. The kids in the camp formed shifting gangs that formed and dissolved, fought and played together; and I soon learned to wait until my brother came home from school so I had an ally and a protector. The Italian family next to us had several children and, while we did play with them sometimes, more often we threw rocks at them over the back fence.

One spring morning I stood outside on the road with my dad and a bunch of other men—the mine was on strike and the men had nothing much to do. I leaned against my dad's legs. He was taller than the other men. They were arguing about the strike. Junie Munro was there with her dad, Hughie, who was big and red faced and English. I stuck my tongue out at Junie who kicked me in the leg. We flew at each other and the men cheered and laughed and formed a circle around us. Junie was older than me. I knew that my mom and dad didn't like Hughie so, even though Junie was older and heavier, I fought for my family and my dad. As we yelled and tore at each other and rolled around on the gravel road, I felt her give in and I rolled over on top of her and began pounding her head into the gravel. One of the men, maybe Junie's dad, pulled me off and made us apologize to each other but I knew my triumph. I knew, from that moment on, that I could win a fight if I had to.

Eventually, my mother found me another friend, a girl who lived up the hill above our house. She was the daughter of the mine supervisor but I didn't know that—I did know I had to climb to her house through the trees and up a long flight of stairs. I was entranced both by these trees, by the grey piped stems of young alders, as well as by the long moss covered flight of stairs in front of her house. Whenever I went to her house, I would climb slowly up and down the stairs several times, loving the feeling it gave me, with no ability to understand why. I had no words for beauty and, since I was alone, there was no one to ask. But something about that place, something about the slender lines of trees next to the grey wooden stairs, the broad yellow flowers of skunk cabbage among the trees, the brilliant multi-shades of green, called me and I responded.

"I hate this place," my mother screamed at my dad almost every night. The winters were long and dark and damp. She couldn't make friends since most of the women in Riondel didn't speak much English. She was pregnant and she didn't want this new baby. She had three small children and we seemed to always have colds from living in the damp basement. We sat inside and stared out the window while rain dripped off the lumber scaffolding on the makeshift roof and leaked in under the front door.

One Sunday afternoon, the tent on the lot next door to us burned. The people got out and the neighbours came running but a canvas tent only takes a few minutes to burn. The ruins of the tent smoked for days while the camp kids, including my brother and I, raked through the warm ashes for the pennies that we heard had been in a jar in the tent.

But the fire upset my mother. The family of several children had barely made it out of the tent alive.

When my sister, Robin, was born that November, the cord was twisted around her neck and she was blue from lack of oxygen. When my mother came home, my small sister cried and cried and my mother cried with her. She hadn't wanted this baby. She had painted the floor of the basement with stinking rubbery paint and the doctor told her this had caused the cord to loosen. He said the baby would be born a monster but instead she was born a tiny girl with a ferocious temper. My brother and I watched from the corner of the kitchen or stayed in our corner room, with the bunk beds and the torn blanket over the door.

My mother couldn't get warm. She stuffed wood in the cook stove that was our only heat and shivered anyway. She was still in her early twenties and now she had four children to care for and no friends. When my father came home she would rage at him and he would rage back. They had moved to Riondel to try to make enough to money to build up a stake so they could go back to farming. But now they were too young and exhausted and the mine didn't pay enough to get them out of the trap of poverty and endless work into which they had fallen.

One night my mother began crying and couldn't stop. My father went outside. A long time later, someone knocked on the door and two men we had never seen before came in with our father. They talked to our mother in low voices and she left with them. Our father glared at us, "Get to bed," he told us.

A few days later my grandmother, my mother's mother, came to stay in the basement with us. She glared at my squalling, red-face baby sister. She snapped at me to help clean up. She sent my brother Bill to his room where he hid, more or less permanently, until she left. When my father came home, she slammed a plate of food onto the table in front of him. My grandmother blamed my father for everything–they didn't even try to pretend they liked each other, but my grandmother fed and cleaned up after us for a long week, until my mother, weak and white and still shivering, finally came home.

Winters in the Kootenays are always dark. The long narrow north-south valleys sock in with clouds in November, a ceiling that doesn't lift until March and the snow that comes is usually wet slush.

Just after Christmas that year it snowed, a deep rug of powdery snow and then, amazingly, the sun came out. Miraculously, this happened on a Sunday and the whole town turned out with cardboard boxes, toboggans and sleighs. Even my mother came carrying Robin, both of them wrapped against the cold. Everyone spent an afternoon sliding down one of the hilly streets. Someone made a fire and someone else donated hot chocolate. When evening came I didn't want to quit. My mother grabbed my hand and towed me reluctantly home but while she was making dinner I slipped out, took my small red sleigh and went back to the hill. In the darkness, I slid and swooped until my father came to find me.

There were a few other bright moments. If the winters were long, the summers were beautiful and there was a long gravelly shallow beach just north of the camp. Some days, in the summer, my father would come home, stooped and dirty from the mine, and we would take our supper to the beach north of town and play in the shallow water until the sun bent the light over the mountains on the other side of the lake and it grew dark.

I always found excuses to follow my father around and one day he took me with him when he went to the farm to visit his father and his step-mother. Their house was old and smelled funny. The only light in the evening came from coal-oil lamps. There was nowhere for me to sleep but curled up on an ancient couch under a blanket. I didn't like my grandfather. He seemed very old and crabby to me. He had rough whiskers and his sweater strained to meet over his belly. When night came, I leaned against my father's knee, missing my mother and wishing we could go home.

"Homesick, eh?" said my grandfather. "Like a baby."

I glared at him with tears in my eyes.

"Look, she's a crybaby."

I looked from him to my father. Both of them were grinning. Even at four I was embarrassed. I had broken some kind of rule I didn't understand. The tears dried into stones. I turned my head away.

Then my father got ill as well. At that time, both of my parents chain-smoked. Everyone did. My father had managed to get himself out of the black depths of the mine, work which he hated and for which he was too tall, and reassigned to loading cyanide laced mine slag on the dock; he hand-rolled his own cigarettes and smoked a toxic combination of lead, cyanide and tobacco. My mother was still far from well. In fact, she had rheumatic fever and was seriously ill but it went undiagnosed for several years.

Chapter One

My grandfather decided to retire from farming and move into Creston. He offered to sell the farm to my parents. They were both homesick for farming, for land and for distance from other people and so, finally, joyfully, we left Riondel behind.

It took us a couple of days to cram everything we owned into our green Dodge pickup. My mother and father, the four kids and our dog Willie, got into the cab and we drove for what seemed forever but was only about an hour and a half. Finally, we turned into a sloping driveway that led to a small cabin squatting under enormous fir trees. The cabin was on the northern edge of my grandfather's farm. It was called Shelackie's cabin after the man who had built it. It had been sitting empty for years. As we all crowded in the door, we were hit by the smell of damp plywood from the always-leaking toilet, mingled with the stink of creosote from the bridge timbers that Louis Shelackie had stolen and used to build it and, underneath that, the reek of packrats.

There were two tiny bedrooms, the kitchen, plus the bathroom. My father set up the bunkbeds and a campbed for Phillip, Bill and I. He set up the ancient gas stove for my mother with its quart glass tank full of white gas. The smell of gasoline added to the reek in the room. That night I kept waking up, listening to the toilet gurgle and the wind smack into the trees over the cabin.

In the morning, my father climbed over the fence and disappeared across the green field below the cabin. In Riondel I had gotten used to being on my own. I liked to wander and no one had the time or energy to worry about it much. I set out to follow him. From the top of the hill, I could see my grandparent's house, but when I got down the hill it was harder going; the grass towered over my head, there was a wide brown creek which meandered between humps of mud and beyond that, a jungle of thistles and ferns with thin trails winding through into darkness. I could see my grandparent's house, but not how to get there. I started into the thistle jungle, where the paths were so narrow the thistles reached out to catch and scratch my bare arms. It was dark in the thistle path and I could no longer see the house. I heard crashing behind me; it was Tiny, the Jersey cow, who my Dad called a muley cow because she had no horns, and the other cow, Bossy, the black and white Holstein, following me through the thistles. I'd met them before; my father had taken us out to the barn and squirted milk in our faces out of their glistening huge bags and thick teats, but my father was far away and the cows were close. I ran as fast as I could, twisting and turning down the many tangled aisles of this enormous jungle, until I spotted the page wire fence, sagging under its burden of brush. I made it over the fence, and into the yard.

My father had seen me coming. He was standing there, laughing at someone so foolish as to be afraid of a couple of cows.

"Cows won't hurt you," he said, "Turn around, stand up to them. Yell at them."

I believed whatever my father said. I stared back at the cows, triumphant now on the right side of the fence and beside my powerful father.

Since I was around, my father did what was most natural to him and found some work for me to do. He said from now on I would have to feed the chickens. If I forgot, he said, the chickens would go hungry and it would be my fault. Bantam chickens dusted themselves and scratched and squatted under every bush. He showed me where the grain was and threw some on the ground. The chickens came running.

From then on, when I went to the shed and got a bucket of grain, chickens came running from all over the yard. They crowded around me, ate what I gave them. I loved their colours, their magnificent glowing iridescent feathers, their red combs and their golden-wise eyes. But mostly I was proud of how they came running, that they followed me and trusted me to feed them. One evening I stood with

Chapter One

my small tin can of wheat at the edge of the yard, staring across the pasture, where the evening sunlight was slanting over the emerald grass. My feet sank into the grass, my head swam in the warm air while the chickens pecked and scratched at my feet. I was home now and I knew it, knew that wherever I roamed, from now on, this land would belong to me and me to it.

The piece of land on which I grew up and have now lived most of my life was once a creek delta, a cedar swamp, an almost flat place at the bottom of the Purcell Mountains. It was cleared by Pierre Longueval, a young French immigrant who, in 1920, bought 160 acres of raw land beside Kootenay Lake and set out to create a farm. Kootenay Lake is a long, broad deep expanse of clear green-blue water, threaded between the Selkirk Mountains on the west and the Purcells on the east. Human inhabitants perch uneasily here, on bits of flat land on the toes of the mountain next to the lake. There are few beaches. The rocks are granite. The forest is dark, mixed fir, larch, pine and hemlock.

Pierre had worked hard to make the farm productive but my grandfather, after he bought the place in 1938, had let things go. He didn't care about fruit trees. He only raised a few pigs. That spring my father began plowing ground and setting out tomato seedlings, thousands of them. My baby sister was now a year old, my brother was two. When my mother wasn't cleaning or cooking or washing the milk things or doing laundry with the wringer washer, she went to help. I was alone with a whole new universe to explore on my own.

The farm work fascinated me. There was a lot to learn. That first summer, I stood beside my father on top of the hay wagon as the labouring horses pulled the wagon up the hill towards the barn. He shouted and slapped the horses; even I could see it was too hard for them. They puffed blasts of air out of their red nostrils; sweat ran in dark streams down their necks and legs. They went slow, slow, their heads down, heaving the wagon in little jerks, until it was below the square hole in the back of the top of the log barn. From there, my father had to hoist the hay up a forkful at a time and stuff it in that hole, where it piled up and up until the whole top of the barn was bulging with hay. My job was to stomp on the hay as it came up in scratchy flying forkfuls into the barn. My father stood below me, his shirt off, the long muscles in his back working and bulging as he lifted and bent again for another load.

And after the work was done, my and my brother's reward was that we got to go to the beach, a golden curving crescent of sand surrounded by water worn granite on the south edge of the farm.

To get to the beach we followed a rutted grassy road that went out of the yard, past the end of the chicken shed where a mysterious black pool of water hid in a fringe of elderberry bushes. Here the creek that trickled through the yard made a wide sandy spot in the road that we splashed through in our bare feet. Then we had to run under the dark cedar trees where clouds of mosquitoes waited to attack and down the long hill to the narrow path above the beach. We learned to whip towels around our ears and shoulders to keep them away.

But there were no mosquitoes at the beach. Instead there was the hot sun smoldering onto the layered folds of granite. The same stream that ran through our yard ran here over the rocks and then gullied the sand into layers, smoothing it into long sandbars at the edge of the water. There were sun and water-worn giant tree stumps that could be turned into pirate ships; or elephants or spaceships and piles of driftwood left from high water. We leapt and raced on the long ropes of logs, surefooted as mountain goats.

In the forest above the beach were small surprising secret rooms, carpeted with moss, in the middle of huge leaning fir trees. One day, excited and guilty, I went into one of these rooms and took off all my

Chapter One

clothes. I lay on the moss, looking up through the trees. Coming into such a place always made me catch my breath and hesitate; something about it drew me in and when I was inside, I fell into a kind of dream. Such a place went somewhere inside me, made me wonder, made me happy. When I lay down in the middle of the moss, I found myself in the middle of a perfect room, a room of silent green happiness. It was a kind of worship, an amazement that there could be such a place and that I could be in it, rolling on the moss and prying the moss apart to watch a tiny miniature world of bugs and ants and dust.

Because we had to go to the beach by ourselves, my mother wanted to make sure we knew how to swim. She didn't have time to come with us every day although she loved the beach and tried to come when she could. At least she knew if we could swim, we wouldn't drown. But I had a yellow inflated duck that I loved to float on, staring down at my peculiar angular feet in the green water, or drifting from place to place, paddling my feet and pretending to be a boat.

One afternoon, when I put on my pink bathing suit and grabbed the duck, my mother took the duck away. "You have to learn to swim," she said.

I stared at her. I knew perfectly well I could swim. I'd already figured it out. Swimming was simple. It wasn't something anyone had to learn; all you had to do was run into the water and kick hard. Dog paddling, we all called it. Except our small black dog Willy wouldn't go in the water at all unless our father picked him up, carried him into the water and threw him in. Then he swam frantically for shore, his head high and his front feet splashing in his desperation.

"I can swim already," I told her but she held my yellow duck over my head. Disgusted, I left the house and went down the long path to the beach. No one else was there. I waded into the water, swam a few strokes and went back up to the house.

"I can so swim," I said. Defeated, my mother handed me the yellow duck and I went back to the beach. I spent the next few weeks paddling around on the duck but my father found out and made fun of me. Toy ducks were for little kids, for babies. I knew my father must be right and, reluctantly, I left it behind on the next trip to the beach.

The first summer flew by; I made friends with the cows. My father's solution of turning around to yell at them worked. I followed them around and let them lick my hands and face with their long gooey sloppy tongues. I followed my father around as well, out to the barn to milk, into the house, stride, stride; if I tried, I could stretch out my legs to match his steps. When I marched behind him, from place to place around the farm, everything obeyed him, everything was ours, except inside the house, where my mother was always working.

Until we moved to the farm, my father had been a distant figure–someone who went to work and came home and caused trouble. On weekends, or occasionally in the summer, he had taken us to the beach or sometime we played outside beside him while he worked in the garden he had made or on the tall picket fence he built to enclose it. But my mother was the center of the house, the center of our lives.

Now, at the farm, everything interesting, joyous, unexpected, magical or mysterious belonged to my father–the chickens, the enormous horses, the cows, the endless trees, the tall grass and thistle fields were my father's and the rules were my father's as well. My mother seemed as trapped as a flightless bird; her children came and went from the house but she stayed in it. I tried to bring her gifts from my new world by telling her stories, or bringing in flowers, or gifts from the gardens or the fruit trees. But more and more I ran after my father, who didn't care what I did as long as I didn't get in the way. And when he was busy or gone, I ran by myself.

For that first summer, the farm was a place of hope, sunshine, a place where my mother sang at her endless work. That August my

Chapter One

father took us out to the tomato field and handed us enormous tomatoes to eat, full and dripping with juice.

And finally, late that first summer, we moved out of Shelackie's cabin and into the farmhouse. Pierre, who we called Pete, had been building the house when he died and my grandfather had done little to finish it. Pete had built it one room at a time, so each of the rooms had a door. And I, finally, for the first time, had a room of my own. Now, every night, I climbed the long stairs in the dark to my room, with its two small windows facing north, where I could look out over the cow pasture. I had a big double bed and a rug on the floor of my room, a hairy rug backed with green felt, which my mother told me had once been the hide of my grandfather's favourite horse. I wasn't sure how I felt having a dead horse on my floor but I both loved and was terrified of my room. Each night I undressed in the middle of the dead horse rug and then leapt for the bed, where I tucked in the blankets to keep myself safe.

The house was dark and spooky. We didn't yet have electricity so our light came from kerosene lanterns that my father lit every evening. My mother and father both joked about Pete's ghost and indeed, doors opened and shut at odd moments. At night, after we all went to bed, the house creaked and snapped as it settled into itself. The tin chimney in the corner of my room that went down to the wood cook-stove whispered and rattled as it cooled or as the wind outside hit it. I could hear my brother and sister breathing in the next room. I could hear the cows lowing in the pasture. And when the windows were open, I could hear the wind coming over the fir trees, I could hear the night birds trilling as they went after mosquitoes and the creek eternally murmuring in its muddy ditch.

But the brief space of peace and hope didn't last. Something happened to the tomato crop that was going to make us so much money. My parents slept downstairs and, lying awake at night that fall, I could hear them arguing, arguing, arguing, their voices rising and falling through the floor as I lay very still, the blankets tucked around my legs, in my dark cold room.

I began to dread sitting down for supper. Every evening when we sat down to eat at a table laden with rich farm food, my parents started in at each other, their voices bitter and deadly. One night my father got so angry he stood up, grabbed the edge of the table laden with food that my mother had just set down, turned it over and stomped out into the night, slamming the door behind him. I was terrified at the sight of our dinner spread across the floor. Finally I began to mop with a towel at the terrible waste of a whole gallon of milk flooding across the worn linoleum but my mother, furiously weeping, yelled at me, told me to leave it, go away, go upstairs and leave her alone to clean up.

The farm work soon claimed both my parents. My mother's day began early in the morning when my father came in from milking at six. She had to make sure the creamer was scalded and ready, then she strained the milk into the creamers and put it in the outside fridge. She had only a woodstove to cook on. My sister was still difficult and fretful. One day in early spring she said, "You're old enough now to help out. Take Robin outside and play with her. Don't let her go near the road."

I stood around for a bit, watching my year and a half old sister tottering around the muddy yard in her bright red snow suit. I didn't like my small sister; she cried a lot and so was annoying. My father was lying on his back under a tractor, taking it apart. I thought Robin would go back inside to our mother if I ignored her, so as soon as no one was looking, I trotted off to the beach. An hour or so later, a car stopped. A neighbour had found my sister heading down the gravel road.

I lied. "I thought Dad was watching her," I said. My mother knew I was lying but she never asked me again to look after Robin.

Chapter One

My brother and sister were my mother's problem and none of mine. Mine was this new kingdom of fields and green glowing rooms under trees and golden water where fish swam and clams full of pearls waited to be opened. Mine was the garden, the new peas and carrots, the apple and cherry trees that could be climbed to the top. My mother tried to catch me, comb my hair, wash my face, but each morning I escaped her, out to the barn or the garden or the beach.

Chapter Two

OUR FARM IS on the eastern shore of Kootenay Lake, which is part of the Kootenay-Columbia River system. The Kootenay-Columbia basin, in the southeastern corner of British Columbia is, in effect, an island, bounded and circled by rivers. The Columbia and Kootenay Rivers both flow out of adjacent valleys in the Rocky Mountains, into the Rocky Mountain Trench. They almost meet at Canal Flats, but then the Columbia River flows north and the Kootenay River flows south, only to both circle around and finally meet again at Castlegar. It is an island that encompasses desert, tundra, alpine, boreal forest, dry pine prairie, alpine lakes and rivers and many small and varied communities of humans spotted along the valley bottoms.

Over the millennia, geographies, people, species and ecological systems have met here and crossed and crossed again. Not once but three times, tectonic plates have collided here, overlapped, creating four different mountain ranges: the Monashees, the westernmost range of the Columbias, the ancient Purcells, the newer Selkirks and the still newer and still growing Rockies. One of the edges of these plates runs down the middle of Kootenay Lake, so that the Purcell Mountains on the east are an older mountain range than the granitic Selkirks to the west.

The first people probably arrived here about 15,000 years ago, after the enormous lakes created by glaciation had a chance to recede. The area had to re-vegetate and gradually it became a steppe-tundra of sage, grass and scattered spruce and fir. Salmon ran from the ocean, all the way up the Columbia River into the lakes, and steelhead and char were abundant in the lakes as well. The people who lived there moved seasonally from valley bottoms and lakeside winter camps to summer hunting terrain in the mountains.

Archeological evidence indicates that the Ktunaxa people, the Shushwap people and the Sinixt people all shared the resources of Kootenay Lake but, for some reason, didn't settle there.

The Ktunaxa people near Creston have been traditionally reluctant to talk to researchers, with good reason: their history of contacts with white people has been the usual litany of misunderstanding and betrayal. The first European person the Ktunaxa encountered in any major way was David Thompson, the explorer whose name is most associated with the Kootenay Region, although other white fur traders had passed through the area.

David Thompson established a trading post on Windermere Lake in 1806 and, in 1811, he was the first European to travel the full length of the Columbia River from its origin at Canal Flats to Astoria near the mouth of the Columbia River and back again.

At this time a race was on between the British and the Americans to discover the source of the enormous river that blasted into the Pacific Ocean at Astoria, Oregon. As the Columbia headed north, Thompson logically assumed it was not the river in question. The Kootenay, flowing south, seemed a more likely candidate.

So, in the following spring of 1808, David Thompson left his wife Charlotte and their children, who followed him on most of his travels, at Kootenae House. He followed the Kootenay River south into Montana, then Idaho, and kept going when it looped north into Canada. He arrived at the south end of Kootenay Lake on May 14, 1808, and met up with a group of Kootenay Lake inhabitants or, as he named them, Marsh or Swamp People, which was not their name for themselves. They called themselves Yaquan Nukiy, which translates as "the place where the rock is standing".

He and his men paddled, accompanied by swarms of mosquitoes, through the reed beds and marshes at the south end of Kootenay Lake. He asked the locals what lay to the north and, instead of telling him there was a lake, they warned him of a series of waterfalls and five portages, one of them twenty miles long. It was a decisive moment and cost Thompson another two years in actually finding the route of the Columbia. His men were out of food so, tired and discouraged, Thompson turned back.

Because all the rivers were in flood, he decided to go overland by horseback. He hired a young Ktunaxa man for a guide, who stayed with them for a couple of days and then left. It's interesting to speculate what the exact route was that he used in getting back to Tobacco Plains; it was most probably along the Moyie River, which flows south from Moyie Lake west and south of present day Cranbrook.

According to Thompson's diary, they had a terrible time, crossing the flooded river in several places by making log bridges. After twelve days of living mostly on bread made from roasted moss and the occasional antelope or deer, they came out into the valley near Columbia Lake.

In May of 1812, David Thompson left the Kootenay area forever. He never did see the great blue stretch of Kootenay Lake. At that time, before the dams, the south end of the lake where he arrived would have been a lengthy maze of bulrushes, swamps, mud and mosquitoes. Maybe that's why he turned south. Or perhaps the locals warned him off because they were afraid of what he would do to the magic—or the magic would do to them. Or maybe they were afraid he'd stick around and never leave.

Growing up, I didn't know anything about First Nations people or First Nations history. Our mother told us various stories in which Indians figured as mysterious people who showed up occasionally. Her best friend was named Louise. When they were about ten, Louise and my mother wanted a horse more than anything; they saved the bits of money they made doing chores for their parents. They took their change, got someone to take them to the reserve, where the Indians sold them a shaggy, wild, half-starved half-grown colt. They led it home while it alternately tried to bite and kick them and tied it in Louise's parent's woodshed. With their last bit of money, they bought a bag of oats. That night, the colt broke the rope, got into the bag of oats and ate most of it. When they came in the morning, the colt was lying on its side, barely breathing. They got it on its feet and walked it around for hours until it recovered. Once the horse got some strength, it turned out to be both wild and vicious so, reluctantly, they sold it back to the Indians.

Indians ran through other tales my mother told and sometimes, when we went into town, we passed a wagon drawn by a team of horses, the adults sitting hunched on the front seat, a bundle of children in the back. I always stared—anything to do with horses caught my interest. Or I would see the teams tied up in a vacant lot on the edge of town, the same dark people standing around, sometimes with a fire going.

Indians always seemed to be far outside the rest of the world and, since I felt I lived there as well, I thought I should know more about them. But it was hard to connect the stories my mother told with the people I saw on the edge of town. I never saw them anywhere else—they weren't in school or in the stores or even on the streets of town. They were just at the edge of things, a glimpse that caught my attention and stayed there simmering.

I knew one of our closest neighbours, Mabel O'Neil, was an Indian because my mother said she was but I also knew her as a warm comfortable presence, a purveyor of warm bread fresh out of the oven, slathered with wild strawberry jam, a woman who said little but was clearly at the center of her family's life.

And very occasionally, on the way with my father to buy hay or other supplies, we would pass the small cluster of houses, a white church and a few cars a mile south of town. My father jerked his thumb towards it. "There's the Mission," he said. I didn't know what that meant, but there were those people again. They seemed so distant—they seemed to have lives about which no one knew anything.

So Indians went on being a mystery and a fascination for me. Gradually I found bits and pieces about Indians in books, but the books didn't help much. Indians in books lived far away, hunted buffalo, lived in tipis, not like the Indians I had seen, huddled at the edge of the white people's new settlement. And yet Indians were clearly something like me; they lived outside, in the woods, with animals, all the things that were important to me, that bounded my new life, that gave it shape and meaning and importance.

By the 1880's, the Kootenay Lake area began to be frequented by Europeans and Americans—mostly prospectors and miners drawn by the lure of silver and gold. Eventually, enormously rich silver strikes brought waves of men seeking fortune, followed by the railways and paddle-wheel steamers. Instant settlements sprang up, Sandon, Kaslo, Ainsworth, Nelson and many others. The CPR and the Great Northern Railway ran competing lines into these places, often high in the mountains or in the middle of dense forest.

When the mining boom died down, orchardists formed the next

wave of immigration. The first orchards were planted in 1890 and from 1910 to 1930 many farms took root around the shores of Kootenay Lake. The east shore was and is a particularly good growing area for cherries, peaches, pears and apples, although almost no one has an orchard these days. Markets are far away and orchards are hard work. Lakeshore is seen as being for recreation, for retirement, for scenery, not for farming.

The mining 'camp' of Riondel was settled because of a silver, lead and zinc mine that, when my dad worked there, was known as the Bluebell Mine. In 1882, an American named Robert Sproule staked four claims along the peninsula, including the Blue Bell. When he left to register his claims, an Englishman, Thomas Hammill, restaked the claims. This led to a dispute that ended with Sproule shooting Hammill dead and going to the gallows for his crime.

In 1905, The Canadian Metal Company purchased the mine and in 1907 the settlement was named Riondel after Count Edouard Riondel, the president of the company.

The mine closed in 1943 and the town was soon empty but, in 1950, the mine re-opened and the population soared to almost 300 within three years. My father and mother moved there in 1952, desperate for a job and money.

Pierre Longueval, the young Frenchman who took up a 160 acre land grant on the edge of this huge cold lake, showed up in 1918, young, ambitious and energetic. I know very little of Pierre, or Pete as he ended up being called. Stories of early beginnings get lost too fast—by the time I thought of writing this book and had the skills to do it, too many of the elders in our community had already died. So the little I do know of Pierre has come down through anecdotes, bits of stories sifting down like dust over the years.

I know he came from France with a group of other settlers; he

Chapter Two

went first to Saskatchewan, then Alberta and then somehow he came to BC, found the lake and took up 160 acres of land. He had money—he was a French remittance man—so that one of the stories with which my siblings and I grew up was that of Pete's hidden gold.

The story in our family was that when my grandfather first came to the Kootenays he sold Pete some hay and Pete went outside, came back in with a jar of gold coins and paid my grandfather. After my younger brother and I heard this story, we crawled under the barn and chicken shed, we dug and explored but we never found the gold.

Pierre died in Kootenay Lake, which even now has a reputation for catching people unawares. Kootenay Lake is not a friendly lake—it is deep and cold, so cold that the bodies of drowned people are not recovered. Squalls can sweep unexpectedly down its long narrow length. And because the wind hits with particular ferocity in the middle, away from the sheltering bays, boats with naïve drivers often leave shore thinking the waves aren't too tall only to meet, farther out, the big rollers driven by the wind roaring down the centre of the lake.

So we know he drowned but we don't know the whole story. We do know that he was tall and good-looking, that he was well-educated, interested in socialism and that he had a girlfriend. He also had a housekeeper, Leontyne Duperron, who had come out from the prairies to get away from the prairie winter and so most of what I know of the story comes from her daughter, Marguerite Duperron.

Marguerite was born in Unity, Saskatchewan. Pierre was a relative of her grandmother's, who had re-married after her first husband, a man called Louis Vasseur who had come to Canada from France with several of his brothers, died. Pierre's parents had also died when he was young and so he came to live with the Vasseurs as a young man. In 1922, Marguerite, her sister, mother, father and Pete all moved to the Kootenays. They spent one winter in a log cabin five miles north of the booming railway town of Sirdar. Marguerite was seven and, every morning, she and her sister got up and trudged three miles along the rutted dirt road, through knee-deep snow, to go to school. They left home in the dark and arrived back again in the afternoon in the dark. But the train engineers got to know them and the train would wait at a lonely railroad siding, called Atbara, a mile from the school, where they could climb gratefully into the warm caboose and ride the last mile.

The next year, Pete bought the property on the lake. He was both progressive and ambitious. He read books and pamphlets on modern agriculture that were still in the house when we moved in. And he must have already had the idea that someday lakeside property might be valuable so, before he built his house, he built two cabins above the shining gold sand beach below the farm. Pete and Marguerite's dad bought a small gasoline-driven sawmill Together he and Pete cut the massive cedars off what is now our pasture and milled out wood for the cabins, the house, a barn, a woodshed and a long, elaborate chicken house with ventilation shafts, roost, nesting boxes and a root cellar underneath.

In the years Pete lived there, from 1922 to 1937, he accomplished an astounding amount. Besides the buildings, he fenced and cross-fenced the property with split-rail fences made of cedar logs. The cedar logs were charred on the outside. My father told me once that Pete would haul the logs to the beach, pile them up, light them on fire and then throw sand on them to put the fire out, a process akin to making charcoal. The charring seems to make them impervious to rot so that some of these fences are still standing and still solid. He kept goats and chickens; he planted an enormous orchard of apples, pears, cherries, plums; he built his house beside the path that would become the road, out of sight of the lake, and my grandfather said that Pete was planning on opening a store when there was more population along the lake.

Pete altered the landscape in other ways; an old rockslide, still barely visible above the highway just south of the farm, was caused by Pete diverting water from one creek into another.

There was no actual road to the farm then, just a track known as the tote road. The road went north from Creston to Kuskanook, where the sternwheelers docked, and then it was a three-mile hike or wagon-ride to the farm. Kuskanook had already boomed and died. Very briefly, Kuskanook had served as the terminus of a branch of the Bedlington Northern Railway. There the cargo and passengers were loaded onto a sternwheeler but, after the railway was finished on the western side the lake, the railbed to Kuskanook was torn up and turned into a dirt road. But people still kept cabins in Kuskanook, at the end of the road, for fishing or boating.

One late fall, Pete had a house party. His girlfriend apparently decided she wanted to go fishing. Pete had a canoe and he and the girlfriend went down to the lake. She came back a couple of hours later with a story that the canoe had overturned, that Pete had called to her to swim for shore, he would be right behind, she was on top of the canoe and he was kicking behind, but he never made it. She climbed up the steep rocks and came back through the trees.

After Pete died, things quickly disappeared from the farm. People came and claimed tools, animals and farm implements, then eventually the farm was sold for taxes. Pete had died in 1937 and, in 1938, my grandfather bought the whole 160 acres for $2525. Someone else had bid $2500.

In 1995, my father, Bill and I tore down the old chicken shed. The huge one-foot by one foot solid squared off beams under the floor had finally rotted through. We saved the wide-grain, old growth cedar lumber from the walls and the sheet metal roofing and burned the rest. We looked through the dusty ground and kicked at the rotten beams but no gold coins appeared.

Pete's dreams still haunt the land; whether his ghost does or not is unknown. When I wander there now, I wonder if he would be pleased or angry at what we've done—or haven't done.

There is another farm in our family history, one I still dream about even though it has long been sold.

When my parents were first married, as a wedding present, my grandfather bought them a farm, five miles south of his farm. It was known then and still, in our family, as the Mannarino place.

The Mannarino place, like most farms along the lake, was a couple of cleared benches of land on the side of the mountain. The farm was located there because of a stream tumbling through it. This farm was at the south end of the lake, above a vast area of swamp, cottonwood trees and thick willow bush. From a few places on the farm, there was a view to the north of the long sweep of water continuing northward out of sight. Just below the farm, cutting through a swath of thick willow and cottonwood, a channel of the Kootenay River ran northward into the lake. A five mile long stretch of railroad track crossed the swamp at the south end of the lake and directed the railway onto the west side of the lake where it ran northwards to where the river flows again out of Kootenay Lake, south past Nelson and then into the Columbia River at Castlegar.

My mother, Dorothy Klingensmith, and my father, Robert Armstrong, had met just after the Second World War. My mother had just returned from working at the Boeing aircraft factory in Vancouver. My father hadn't gone to war; his father wangled an exemption for him as an essential farm worker.

My mother's grandfather was one of the first settlers into the valley. Her paternal grandfather, my great grandfather, had moved to Creston from Pennsylvania. Although his family was settled and fairly wealthy in Pennsylvania, with a feed mill and a sawmill, he began searching for oil in the early 1800's. Eventually he wound up working for the Canadian Pacific Railroad as a sawmill superintendent; finally he settled on ten acres in Erickson. There he built a three-story southern-style house, with a wide verandah, shaded windows and an enormous kitchen and dining room. The verandah

Chapter Two

wrapped around three sides of the house; the huge dining room and living room were lined with books and gloomy black and white photographs of people. Upstairs there was secret room behind the walk-in closet between the master bedroom and the second bedroom.

My grandfather, Fred Klingensmith, grew up with a strict stepmother who, according to my mother, beat him with a strap. Whatever the reason, he was a man who was not much interested in family and much more interested in finding the elusive gold mine for which he searched his whole life. He met my grandmother in a mining town in northern Ontario.

My maternal grandmother, Lucy Rhinehart, had come to Canada on her own when she was eighteen. She was a woman of independent spirit who had first run away from her family in Liverpool to an aunt in Sweden when she was only twelve. In Canada, she took a job cooking in the small northern mining town of Temiskaming, where she met Fred Klingensmith, who was working in the sawmill. They moved to Port Huron where their first child, my aunt Aileen, was born, then back to Creston, where Fred's parents were. He got a job as a filer in the local sawmill.

My grandparents had five children and my mother was the second youngest. My grandfather wasn't much of a provider or a father. His real love was prospecting and when he wasn't working he was roaming the mountains looking for gold.

One story my mother often told us was about a time he took a job in Nakusp, a town at the northern end of the Kootenays, on the upper Arrow Lake. My grandmother would take her brood of children and they would travel there on the sternwheeler, setting off from Creston, traveling the length of Kootenay Lake to Nelson, then getting on the train to Castlegar and off and onto another sternwheeler, and then travelling the Arrow Lakes to Nakusp.

Along the way they would eat in the dining room where the

tables were set with white linen and silver tableware and tall black stewards in white coats with white gloves waited on them with grave courtesy, before showing them to their cabins to sleep.

But once they had been longer between visits than usual. When they arrived at Nakusp, the children ran to meet their father, who turned to the man he was walking with and asked in bewilderment, "Who are those children?"

My mother grew up in a large white house in the middle of Creston, a half a block from Canyon Street, the main thoroughfare that runs through the centre of the town. Creston was a new town. It sits on a slope above where the Kootenay Lake wetlands used to be. Creston is at the centre of a large flat and fertile area suitable for orchards, cattle or growing hay. As soon as settlers arrived they began changing the landscape as fast as they could, clearing land, planting orchards and strawberry fields. But what really drew their eye was the vast expanse of swamp below the town. It was gradually dyked off and turned into farmland.

Creston also acquired the nickname of Little Chicago. It was a rough brawling town, close to the US border, divided by the railway track that ran below Canyon Street. The better class of people lived up the hill, while the bars and the poor people were literally below the tracks.

When my grandfather lost his job during the depression, my grandmother opened a boarding house. And then my grandmother got sick. She developed bowel cancer. My mother was only twelve but she quit school to help with the cleaning and cooking. My grandmother went to Vancouver for a risky operation but survived and came home.

When the war broke out, my mother went to Vancouver and lived with her Aunt Diz. Her real name was Daisy but her family called her Dizzy. She lived up to the name. Her husband, Murdoch McLeod was an optometrist who travelled to all the little towns in the

Chapter Two

Kootenays to fit people with glasses. They had nine kids. The house was chaos most of the time because Aunt Diz really wanted to be a concert pianist and would practice the piano all night, especially, according to my mother, whenever Murdoch came home. During the war, my mother got a job at the Boeing Aircraft Factory carrying rivets around. For the first time in her life, she could indulge herself in her real passion, which was music, and she began taking singing lessons on weekends along with her brother Charlie. Her singing teacher told her she had a fantastic soprano voice and she could become an opera star. He asked her to move to Toronto with him to study at the Toronto Conservatory.

When the war ended, she desperately wanted to go on with her singing career but she had no money once her job at Boeing ended. She went home to Creston to ask her family for money and they refused her. My grandmother told her she was being foolish to even dream of such a thing. Instead, she got a job in the Mercantile store and met my father.

My father was born in southern Saskatchewan, in the small town of Central Butte. His father, William Armstrong, had been born in Markham Ontario and had married a sensitive, artistic young woman named Winifrith Browne, whose nickname was Queenie. She agreed against all sense and counsel, to move west with him and go wheat farming in Saskatchewan. She had one child who died in infancy and then she had three more children: my aunt Jean, my father, and then their sister Helen. And then, tragically, my grandmother Queenie died of cancer when my father was seven, in 1931, just as the 'dirty thirties', a combination of drought and depression, were hitting the prairies. My grandfather hired an eighteen year old local girl, Helen Nelson, as a combination nanny and housekeeper and then he loaded everything he thought he needed in a steamer trunk, pulled the back seat out of his car, loaded in the steamer trunk and, with the three kids and Helen perched on the trunk, he headed back to Markham, Ontario. They all spent the winter with his parents but something went wrong and in the spring, Grandpa Armstrong headed back to Central Butte, Saskatchewan. He stayed long enough to take off a crop of wheat and then the steamer trunk went back in the car, his land went up for sale and he headed for Creston, British Columbia, where he had a friend who was the manager for the Bank of Commerce. Grandpa knew he could get a loan to buy land and start again.

Armstrong men are famously tough and hard to get along with and both my father and my grandfather were no exception to this. My paternal grandfather Armstrong was descended from the Armstrong clan, who lived along the border between Scotland and England. The Armstrongs were one of the most famous of the so-called "riding" clans, the Reivers or thieves, who fought with both the English, the Scots, their neighbours and, when they ran out of people to fight with and steal from, each other. The Armstrongs were the most feared riding clan on the frontier, riding small but tough black horses. They lived up in the hills, where the pasture was thin and farming difficult,. When they needed to, they swam their horses across the rivers to steal what they needed to survive. The Armstrongs knew the hills and passes intimately. They knew where to hide themselves, and their stolen cattle, often in the bogs or swamps in the valleys.

Reivers were given to feuding and often vicious to outsiders or to each other. There are lots of romanticized legends and stories about the Reivers. For example, one story is that when the women of the household felt that supplies were running low, they would place a covered plate before the men. When the top was taken off, there would be a pair of spurs on the plate. The message, to ride or to starve.

The Armstrongs stayed independent even of the church. Bishop Leslie, a historian, wrote in 1572 that "their [Borderers] devotion to their rosaries was never greater than before setting out on a raid and, on the Scottish Border, it was the custom of christening to leave unblest the child's master hand in order that unhallowed blows could be struck upon the enemy." When the Bishop of Liddesdale came for a visit to one Armstrong household, he demanded: "Are there no Christians here?"

"Na, we's be a' Elliots and Armstrangs," was the answer.

Reiving, or thieving was for winters when food was scarce. Some of the raids would consist of a large group of men and could last for days. Smaller raids might be a moonlight ride, a quick plunder and disappear back to their homes. Whether the raid was a full-scale invasion for political reasons or a raid against a single farmhouse, reiving was a daring and difficult business. Reiver's needed to be fast, strong and tough as nails. The Clan Armstrong motto reflects this. *"Maneo Invictus"* meaning *"We remain unvanquished."* You can kill an Armstrong, but you can't defeat him.

The first Armstrong of my family to come to Canada was William Armstrong. In 1817, William left his village of Hirsthead, in Cumberland, and came initially to New York with his cousin, James Elliot. In 1825, he bought 195 acres of land in Markham, Ontario. His father Thomas, his mother Elizabeth and six other siblings, one brother and five sisters, also came to Canada. Thomas didn't live long but Elizabeth lived to the, then astonishing, age of 89. William married Esther Reesor in 1833 and they produced eight children. Their son, Robert Goodfellow Armstrong was my great great-grandfather.

The Reesors were a clan of devout Mennonites who had come to North America in 1739, after being persecuted in Europe. Initially they settled in Pennsylvania but, in 1786, Peter Reesor settled on six hundred acres of land in Upper Canada. In 1804 the rest of his extended family made the journey northwards in five Conestoga wagons. The six families bought land in Markham and became prosperous farmers. I have often wondered at the odd coincidence of settlement that created a relational bond between a clan of wild thieves and a clan of devout pacifist Mennonites.

When my parents met, my father was living on the farm on the lake by himself and looking after it for his father. He began spending a lot of time bicycling the twenty miles of rutted muddy road to Creston in order to see my mother.

In their wedding picture, my parents look extraordinarily young, beautiful and hopeful. My father is tall and handsome, with black hair and dark brown eyes set back under strong brows. His jaw juts out; his eyes are intense. He is a big man, six feet and four inches tall, with huge broad shoulders and enormous spatulate hands. My mother is tiny beside him, a foot shorter, her soft brown hair curled on her shoulders, her eyes wide and serious. They married on the long weekend in May 1945, and for their honeymoon, they went to Alberta, to a ranch then owned by my grandfather's brother, a huge ranch in the Cypress Hills called the East and West Ranch.

And then they went to work as farmers.

My parents were both used to hard work. My mother, as a teenager, was in charge of cooking and cleaning for five or six men while her mother was ill. My father's first paid job was at twelve, running a combine, but he had been working for his father and living more or less on his own since he was eight.

When they married, my father was 21 and my mother was 23. They were intensely in love. They had the farm, plus a team of horses and a few tools. My father wanted to be a farmer; it was what he knew and I don't know if he ever considered any other choice. Plus he and my mother wanted to be alone; they were both shy and not terribly social. Most of their lives they avoided society, didn't join groups or go to church, partly because they didn't have time and partly because they weren't any good at it. They seemed to have no social ambitions although they got on well with all their neighbours and gave away endlessly generous and bountiful amounts of food.

At first my father adored my mother. After a hellishly lonely life, finally he had someone to love and someone who loved him. Sexuality was an amazing discovery for both of them; my mother told me later, when I was old enough to understand, that sex was the thing that always kept them together, despite a lifetime of bitter fighting.

Neither of my parents had ever gone out with anyone before. My father wasn't at all interested in sharing this new love with someone else, certainly not with a baby. But of course my mother became pregnant almost immediately and she very much wanted children.

The Mannarino place was three miles north of the small railroad town of Sirdar and fifteen miles north of Creston. It had first been cleared and settled by Jimmy and Victoria Mannarino, hence the name. Jimmy had built a white clapboard house with a broad verandah; across the yard was a corral, two log barns and, just below the house, he had planted an orchard with grape vines and prune trees. The nearest neighbours were James and Lillian Wilson to the south, who lived along the old tote road that ran above the highway. James and Lillian's son, Charles, and his new wife, Muriel, lived in a cabin about half a mile away. Dorothy and Gene Haines farmed about a mile to the north along with their son, Mike, who was the same age as my dad. Muriel and Mom had children at about the same time; Charlie and Muriel's son, Clive, was a bit older than my brother Phil; their second son, Alan, was born three months after me. One of the first pictures I have of myself is of Alan and I sitting together in a crib on the screened porch of the house on the Mannarino farm.

Three miles away, at Sirdar, there was a clan of people who had come here from the village of Petilia Policastro in Italy. These were the Pascuzzos, the Lombardos, the Cherbos and Jimmy Mannarino, who settled away from the others.

My parents had never known the Mannarinos but they had heard stories, lots of stories. Jimmy was apparently more than a little hard to get along with. He was not very tall, only about 4 ft. 10 in., but he fought with people. Jimmy had a silver mine up on the mountain above his farm; he also had a mining partner named Pedro Cherbo. Just a few years ago, Mike Haynes told me the story of Jimmy and Pedro's gunfight. He said they got along well until Pedro got the idea that maybe the mine should be all his and he should get rid of Jimmy.

This was in the late 1920s, when the CPR was building the railway across the lake. Pedro told Jimmy he had gotten someone from the railway crew to stash a few cases of dynamite in the brush beside the tracks. As they were going down the hill single file along the path to the railway, Pedro pulled his pistol and shot Jimmy in the back. The pistol apparently had a terrific pull to the right, so Pedro missed Jimmy's heart and got him in the shoulder. Jimmy fell to the ground and Pedro tried to shoot him in the head but missed. Jimmy played dead and Pedro ran away. When he was gone, Jimmy got up and staggered off along the railway tracks to Sirdar to get help.

Pedro holed up in the log barn up beside the Mannarino's house and when a posse of men showed up led by Constable Bill Crawford from Creston, they proceeded to shoot it out. Pedro had his pistol and a 25-35 Winchester rifle. But eventually he ran out of ammunition and had to give up.

Jimmy died of old age and Victoria Mannarino, who was much younger than her husband, sold the farm to my grandfather. My mother and father moved into the beautiful old house. They were determined to make a go of it as farmers. There were two enormous log barns north of the house, one of which still had the bullet holes in it. My parents planted a huge garden and began bringing back the orchard, pruning the trees, deer fencing and cross fencing the

Chapter Two

pasture. There were a lot of varieties of what would now be called heritage trees, such as Black Republican cherries and Northwest Greening apples. There were even two mulberry trees and a huge garden, all ditch irrigated out of the stream that ran down the gully in front of the house from a big concrete tank up in the trees. This too was terraced with beautifully built rock walls.

They had a team of horses and every summer my father cut marsh grass for hay across the river, floated it across the river on a raft, and hauled it up the long steep hill with the labouring team. What they hadn't realized, and no one had told them, was that the farm was directly above an enormous swamp that flooded in the spring. After the water went down and the nights warmed up, mosquitoes came out of the swamp in vast hellish clouds, but the work still had to be done. The garden had to be watered, the fruit picked, the hay gotten in, and wood cut for winter. My mother canned fruit and vegetables and venison. She learned to shoot grouse and spear bass in the river. But after my oldest brother was born, they realized they could no longer live on grouse and venison. They tried to make money from the orchard and the garden but it wasn't enough. The next spring, my father got a job working on the dikes that were built on the Creston flats.

Because it was a long drive home over bad roads, my father often stayed over in Creston during the week and came home on weekends. My mother was left alone in an isolated farmhouse with a new baby. The farm was a small clearing in a vast, mostly untouched wilderness. Below the farm were hundreds of acres of swamp and above the farm was mountains and forest. The bears came regularly to raid the orchard and the deer wandered through what had always been, to them, home.

One night something woke her. She sat up and was terrified to see a white shape in the doorway of her bedroom. Fortunately, she had the baby in bed with her, but she sat up all night in terror wondering what this thing was she was seeing. The next day my father came home and she told him what had happened. So that night when they went to bed they waited and sure enough, the same white shape, the shape of a little bent over old man with a cane, appeared. In the days before he died, Jimmy had gotten very bent by rheumatism and used to walk with the aid of two canes. Apparently, even with the canes, he used to hoof it the three miles to Kuskanook just to watch the girls go swimming.

They saw this white shape many times after that. They had no idea what or who it was. After a while they just called it Jimmy. At first it frightened them and they tried to find some kind of explanation for it but, as time passed and they saw it often, on both moonlit and dark nights, in various parts of the house, they got used to it. One night my father walked right through it. He says it was kind of cold and the shape wavered apart and came back together again. Nevertheless, he still maintains that he does not believe in ghosts and he has no explanation for the shape that they saw in the house.

Eventually my parents got tired of starving on the Mannarino place and they moved away to Riondel because the mine had reopened and my father could get work. My parents had no intention of permanently leaving this farm and my father made the long thirty-five mile drive as often as he could to look after the trees. They had to leave the horses behind as well. Before they left, my father somehow got the money together to buy enough trees to plant a new orchard. Then he made a desperate and heroic final effort to fence the newly planted orchard with a fence with six strands of barbed wire to keep out the deer in the upper field above the house. But leaving a house and land alone in those days wasn't a good idea. Tools and other things disappeared and someone left the deer fence gate open and deer destroyed the new orchard despite my father's efforts. It was the first time that the land broke their hearts, but it wasn't the last.

Chapter Three

OUR LAND BESIDE Kootenay Lake had a lot more going for it as a farm than the Mannarino place. It was mostly flat, at least below the highway, and the mosquitoes in the summer, though bad, weren't as mind-numbingly terrible as they were at the Mannarino place. There was an orchard just above the lake with about thirty cherry trees, along with many apple, plum and pear trees. On the north of the house, there was a swampy pasture, a log barn and a hayshed, and on the south, the huge chicken shed and more fruit trees. My grandfather had kept pigs and, soon after we moved to the farm, my father acquired two milk cows and a Farmall tractor.

After we moved into the huge dark green farmhouse, mornings at the farm were announced by the rattle of the stove lids on the wood cook-stove in the kitchen downstairs, as my father rose at five to build a fire and then go out to milk. I'd hear the rattle of the bucket as he went across the yard, then fall back to sleep. It wasn't a reassuring sound. It meant that when he came back in, he'd pound on the stairs and, if we didn't get up, he'd come upstairs, drag the covers off and haul our lazy useless asses out of bed.

For, as we were now discovering, the name of the farm was work, and we were its servants. And whatever was to be done, we children were part of its doing. We picked fruit, gathered eggs, pitched hay, fed the chickens, carried in wood. Inside the house, our mother was washing, cooking, cleaning, canning, and sterilizing the milk coolers that sat in the fridge on the back porch. Once a week, she got out the wringer washer, filled it full of hot water from the tap, ran load after load of clothes through the wringer into a galvanized tub, carried them outside and hung them on the clothesline then mopped the puddles that ran all over the floor. On laundry days, the windows misted over and the house smelled damp and sad and grey.

Outside our father was milking, feeding cows, pruning trees, picking fruit, cutting, turning, raking, hauling hay into the barn, hoeing the weeds out of the garden, hauling irrigation hoses from place to place, cutting wood, splitting and stacking wood. The work was seasonal but always endless. Spring was for pruning, raking, burning, plowing the fields and the garden, picking rocks out of the fields; summer was an orgy of picking, canning, freezing fruits and vegetables; fall was killing time, when the pigs, the steers and the chickens went into the freezer, when trees fell to the chain saw and the dead corn stalks rattled, desolate, in the garden. Winter was a brief pause in the frenzy but the cows and chickens still had to be fed and cared for, wood carried into the house and ashes carried out and three meals a day prepared, eaten and cleaned up after. Once when I managed to get up the nerve to ask why we all had to work so hard, my father looked at me.

"You work or you starve," he said.

But for me the farm had two names; if one was work, then the other was freedom and I escaped from one into the other as often as I could. I was crafty at this, as all children are. For example, I loved fishing, and I soon learned that fishing looked like work but was really a matter of

Chapter Three

lying on a rock for an afternoon staring into the depths of the water, watching the golden bodies of squawfish arrow from one nook and cranny to another. Hauled into the light, they were a disappointment, grey, gasping and slimy. Sometimes I managed to catch a trout instead, for which I was inordinately praised by my mother, trout being a change from our diet of chicken, beef and pork. But when I came home, I snuck from the sunshine and cool mystery of the lake into a house charged with anger and despair. For there was still no money, no money, no money. I lay in bed at night in my white bedroom over the kitchen, the only kid with my own room, and listened to my parents' voices vibrate through the floor. Sometimes I'd hear the door slam as my father stormed out of the house. So I escaped whenever I could and the place to which I escaped was the O'Neils.

It was late afternoon on a spring day just after we moved to the farm. I heard a crashing wave of noise, looked up and saw horses running through our yard. In retrospect, there were probably only four or five horses plus a couple of cows, but at the time it seemed like a whole lot more. My father was waving his arms in fury.

There were two girls with the horses. The girls were older than me. They waved back at my furious father; one of them waved at me, and then they were gone. I ran into the house to find out who they were. My mother never answered my question. Instead, she and my father launched into some tedious story about the O'Neils and all their kids and how Dick was Irish and had once been a schoolteacher but now he was a logger. But Mabel was lovely, said my mother, and all those kids, and how did Mabel stand it. But none of this mattered to me. I wanted to know about the horses.

The next day I walked barefoot over the mile of graveled road between our place and theirs. The gravel was burning hot. When I got there the whole family was out weeding the corn patch. They didn't seem surprised to see me.

After the corn was done, the two girls, Nora and Shirley, took me down to the barn. Even at five, I knew this was a wonderful place. They had a barrel with a saddle on it tied between two rafters. We played on that for a while but I wanted more.

We went into the pen where the horses were. There was a big white workhorse named King who stepped on my bare foot. I didn't say anything although my foot felt like it had been hammered flat. I thought if I complained or cried they might make me leave. There was a brown mare named Lady, a small black mare named Gypsy and a shaggy pony named Billy. They put me on Billy and led me around for a while then left me on my own. Billy immediately put his head down and began eating grass. Nora handed me a thick stick and said, " Here, hit him with this."

I did—which got his attention. It was my first riding lesson.

I spent the rest of that summer on horseback. I now know that no parent in his or her right mind would have let us ride those horses. They bit, kicked, bucked and ran away. But I didn't know enough to be afraid, and Nora and Shirley had learned to be tough. My parents were far too busy to notice what we were doing. My mother had my baby sister and brother and all the housework plus gardening, canning, cooking and looking after the milk things. My father was putting up hay, picking fruit and working at the sawmill to make money to support the farm.

Nora and Shirley were the youngest kids of the large O'Neil family. When I met them, Nora was nine and Shirley was eight. Nora was the leader; she had short curly hair, and sparkling dark eyes. My mother always said, "That girl is sly, I don't trust her."

So, of course, I believed everything Nora said. Shirley was beautiful, with long black hair, and my brother Phil developed an immediate crush on her. I never did meet them all. There were two older brothers, Art and Jack, who still lived at home and who logged the mountains with their dad. There were three older sisters who came home occasionally, and at least one brother or perhaps two who had drowned in Kootenay Lake in a canoeing accident. At the time none of this mattered to me. What mattered were the horses, the smell of sun on shiny horsehide, the gripping on to the neck as we slid down a graveled hillside, took the horses down to the beach and made them swim, or trotted home behind the O'Neil's milk cow, which had to be rounded up every night.

Dick and the two boys, Arthur and Jack, logged the hillsides around our farm with the big kindly white workhorse whose name was King. They also bought and sold horses and cattle. They used to get some of their horses by rounding up what was left of a wild herd up north in the Columbia Valley. They'd bring them home in a truck, tie them in the corral, bring them water and feed and when they were reasonably quiet, then Jack or Art would get on, ride them until they quit bucking, and then give them to us kids to ride.

They bit and kicked sometimes, but they never bit and kicked me. After a while, I got to ride Gypsy, who was little and black with a white blaze. She bucked everyone off except me. We had no saddles and only a collection of old and tattered bridles or sometimes ropes tied onto the side rings of a halter.

During our second year at the farm, I begged and pleaded until Dad let me keep a brown mare named Lady at our place. He complained about it but my father complained about everything.

"Horse'll starve a cow," he growled, "and a sheep will starve them both."

I had no idea what he meant. I was just deliriously happy to have a horse. Lady was hard to catch but I'd learned from the O'Neils to hide the bridle behind my back, bring some oats, get her in a corner, get a hand on her side, watch that she didn't kick, get a hand on her mane and slide a bridle rein around her neck. I'd have to find a rock to stand on so I could slip the bit into her mouth and the bridle over her ears. Then I'd have to find a bigger rock and lead her up beside it.

She'd sidle away while I made a flying leap for her back. After a while I learned to fling myself up from the ground onto her back with a kind of scissors kick, hauling desperately on her black thick mane while she ran off. Then I sat up straight, picked up the reins and away we went. Together we went up the mountain or down to the beach or along the road or up the logging track to the O'Neils.

I spent hours with Lady tied to a tree in the yard, cleaning and brushing her. I fed her apples and oats stolen from our chickens. When she was out in the pasture, stretched out in the sun, I curled between her legs, my head on her belly.

I had the O'Neils in my life for two brief years but those years were enough to establish many of the inclinations that have stayed with me through the rest of my life. I liked being at the O'Neil's, so I spent more and more time there. I liked how they lived. No one there seemed to care what I did. I liked everything about it: the barn, the horses, the shed full of interesting junk and the log cabin where they all lived. The cabin squatted under the giant cedar trees beside the waterfall where Twin Bays Creek crashed down the mountainside and ran through the birch and poplar behind the cabin

There were chores at the O'Neil's, but they didn't feel like chores. One day, while we were wandering the mountainside in search of wild strawberries, Nora suggested I move in with them. It made sense to me.

We got on the horses and rode to my parents' house. As I remember it, and as my mother retells it, my parents were in town together, a rare occurrence, and the house was empty. My brothers and sister must have gone with them.

I was only in first grade and couldn't write properly, so I printed out the letters as Nora dictated them, telling my mother I had left home.

We fled on the horses, giggling with daring, giddy with escape, high and free and full of ourselves. That night there was a party of sorts in the O'Neill's log cabin. I lay between them on the mattress in

Chapter Three

the little room off the kitchen with Nora and Shirley telling me dirty jokes that I laughed at without having a clue what they were about. God knows where everyone else slept. I had never spent much time in the house. This was the first time I'd stayed over or even had dinner there. Dinner had consisted of slices of venison and homemade bread with wild strawberry jam.

My parents came to get me late that night. My mother was crying. I didn't really want to go home and I couldn't figure out why she was so upset.

After that I wasn't allowed the same freedom, although I still went riding whenever I could. But I couldn't go home with Nora and Shirley when they came by with the herd of horses and cows. I had to stay in and do the dishes. I hated doing the dishes. I hated being in the house. Everything I did with the O'Neils had an air of daring and wildness, like the afternoon Nora had beckoned to me. "Come on," she had said impatiently. I followed her down the leafy path to the outhouse. She pulled a pack of cigarettes and some matches from her pocket. We all lit up and puffed away. It seemed a bit silly to me but it was important to them and we giggled hysterically at our daring.

My English grandmother, my mother's mother, often came to stay with us. I had been her favourite when I was a baby—I was named after her, Lucy Anne shortened to Luanne — but now nothing about me pleased her. I never combed or washed my hair if I could avoid it. I had no manners. I was like a "wild Indian" she said. This of course was a term that pleased me immensely, though I still wasn't sure what Indians were. But I was convinced by now that free and wild were the best things to be.

I have few photos of myself as a child; in one, taken soon after we moved to the farm, I am standing on the front lawn under the walnut tree wearing a dress and, even though the photo is black and white, whenever I look at the photo I remember that the dress was pink and the satin ribbon tied around my waist was also pink. The photo shows me standing self-consciously, my chin pressed down to my chest. My hair then was long and blond. My mother had combed it into ringlets and tied these with a pink ribbon, shining in the sun. I was self-conscious because this was my first new fancy dress. My grandmother had bought it for my seventh birthday. My mother made a big fuss over this dress, my first party dress. She wanted me to be grateful to my grandmother and I was. But I hated the dress.

I stood there as stiffly and carefully as I could, trying to live up to that dress. It was the first time in my life I felt the terrible gravity and falseness that came from wearing special clothes and being told I looked pretty; it was frightening and pleasing at the same time. I pushed my chin into my chest in an effort to do as I was told, to stand up straight and stop fidgeting, to live up to the importance of the dress. But all I wanted to do at that moment was run away.

In all other pictures I have of myself as a child I am in jeans, sometimes on horseback, once sitting on the ground in the orchard in spring with my arms wrapped around the neck of the O'Neil heifer, called that because we bought her as a calf from the O'Neil's. My hair is either in braids or flying away in tangles.

When I was born my grandmother made me her pet, to the exclusion of the other children, and she bought me special presents. She wanted me, she said, to be a lady. But by the time I was photographed in that dress I had already had most of the experiences that would shape me, met the land, met the forest and the mountains, met the O'Neil kids and their horses. I had learned much from them, had climbed cliffs, had clung on to Nora's waist while the horses slid down the rotten, pea-shaped granite gravel on the mountain north of the farm, had jumped out of the hay loft in the barn because Nora told me I could. I had gone wild and there was no saving me, though my grandmother tried.

My grandmother had been a bit of a wild girl herself. She liked to tell us how she had made it all the way from Liverpool, England, to her aunt in Sweden, on her own; how she had come to Canada and survived by getting jobs as a cook in mining and logging camps. But as my grandmother got older, she became more proudly English. She always called England the mother country. The longer she lived in Canada the more genteel she became, until she had made herself over into a middle-class English gentlewoman, the same fate she had picked out for me.

My grandmother had disapproved of my mother's marriage. She took one look at my father and his father and realized they were beneath her, they had no class, they were rough farmers and uncouth.

But she didn't know what she was up against in the struggle to keep me like her. She knew nothing of farming or horses or half-wild, half-native girls who could curse and stay out as late as they wanted. Although she was a hard worker herself, she didn't understand my father's and his father's ways; rough men, men who worked insanely hard, who matched their strength against the land, determined to best it, men who belched as they settled in their chairs for a nap after lunch, men who swore, men who had no time or patience for manners or prettiness.

I never understood until much later in my life why my grandmother was so angry with me, why I went from being her favourite to being someone she barely noticed and often wouldn't even look at. I missed her and I missed being her pet. I loved my grandmother and, as a child, I expected her to go on loving me, to even share in my delight at my new life and adventures. It was the first time in my life that someone openly disapproved of who I felt I had to be, that someone disparaged and made fun of what I loved with my whole being.

My grandmother lost me to a place and a way of life she considered despicable; she had lost me to Canada, to the woods, to the Kootenays, to forests and trees and bantie chickens and the rough harsh ways of my father. But it wasn't until I became a grandmother myself that I understood the nature of her hurt—she had given me what gifts she could, the gifts she knew, that meant everything to her and I had scorned them. She had tried to tell me the wisdom she had learned in her life and it meant nothing to me. We had loved each other and never understood each other; our different histories, my new culture, her old culture, and my seduction into this new land made us strangers.

I don't know what happened to the dress. I never wore it again. We were so poor. It must have gotten used again. But on the other hand, it was utterly impractical, too frilly for school, too pink and fluffy to withstand much wearing. But I think it hung in my closet for a long time, unworn, reproachful and unloved.

My grandfather had sold us only half of the original 160 acres of the farm. The rest he kept and subdivided for summer cottages. One day when I went to one of my favourite moss rooms, it was gone. The trees were cut down and the moss had shriveled in the sun. I went away and said nothing. I knew no one would care or understand. After that I avoided even going past the new cabin, rising from lumber and sawdust and the shrieks of saws.

People from Creston, a lawyer, a doctor, a pharmacist and other people with money, bought the lots in the subdivision next to our farm and began putting up cabins. Now we, plus the O'Neils, had to share the beach with these new people and their kids, as we called them, the beach kids. We tried to play with them and make friends but their rules were different than ours or, rather, they actually had rules and we didn't. They weren't allowed to swim out into the deep water or dive off the rocks or go in the water until an hour after lunch.

When we came to the beach, we would march past them into the water, swim out as far as we could go and stay out well over our heads, lolling around and spouting like playing whales. Or we'd swim around the rocky point and hide in the rocks deliberately out of sight. Sometimes they sent someone in a boat to check up on us. Then one day a delegation of mothers came up the hill to the farmhouse to complain to my mother that we shouldn't be allowed to come to the beach by ourselves. It was burden on them, these women said, to have to worry about us.

My mother was polite. She would speak to us, she said. But when she told us this story, we all laughed at them together, those timid town people, who were afraid for us. My mother was a wonderful mimic and she made them ridiculous, those mincing prissy women, who had the nerve to criticize her wonderful children. She was proud, she told us, of how independent we were, and we in turn were proud of our toughness and our freedom.

The year I turned eight the O'Neils moved away. I couldn't believe they were going. I went up to their place after they'd left. I went through the empty barn and the line of sheds that stood between the barn and the house. I looked in the windows of the house. Then I walked the trail home through the woods where we had so often ridden, an old skid trail that went up and over the powerline and down through a secret mossy gully between two humpy rocks, through the trees, then down the hill, across the highway, through Sawdust Bay, along the lakeshore and finally home.

I begged and begged and one day my father drove me to where the O'Neils had moved and left me there for a whole weekend. But I didn't understand anything that was going on. Mabel had a new baby and was busy. Jack and Art were still living at the house but working in town. Nora and Shirley didn't want to go riding. They still had horses but they had lost interest in them. We didn't even go down to the barn, just wandered around the fields and went down to the river, played along the logs and sandbars.

That night, as I lay next to Shirley and Nora in the loft of the log house, I could hear cars coming and going, voices downstairs, laughter, loud laughter. I heard a woman screaming.

"Shhh," Nora said. " Don't let them know you're here." I had no idea what she meant. We all lay there pretending to sleep.

The next morning, finally, we did go riding. We went down the road to some neighbours where a group of kids were practicing to ride in the local parade. Nora looked at me critically and said, " Can't you do something about your hair?" I sat miserably behind her as we trotted down the road, trying to comb my hair with my fingers.

That afternoon my father came to get me and I ran to meet him. For the last couple of hours, I had been sitting on the corral fence, sulking and kicking my feet.

I didn't see Shirley and Nora for years after that. Their betrayal hurt hugely but it didn't really matter. They had given me a greater gift. Every night I put myself to sleep dreaming of horses, wild horses. Whenever I had something difficult to do, I imagined myself on horseback. When I needed to push myself, when I needed strength, endurance, when I needed to be both strong and yet careful, I imagined myself free, powerful, in control, riding.

Chapter Four

AFTER THE O'NEILS LEFT, I found another place to escape to that held a different kind of freedom. I found books, reading and writing. After the first summer at the farm, I started school at the small one room school-house in Sirdar, seven miles south of the farm. Sirdar is one of the many small places in the Kootenays that had a few brief bright days when it looked as if it might become something, an important place, a town or even a city. Once it had several hotels and a train station, a railway turntable and a water tower. Most of those things were still there when we were kids but deserted; the railway station, with its rows of seats, its wooden platform, its carefully lettered sign, its window for the ticket agent, was closed and locked. Even though we pressed our noses to the glass of the waiting room, we never broke in. There was something forbidding about the place.

That first school day in September, my older brother and I stood outside the gate beside the road. I wore a new dress and new white and black saddle-shoes. I had a yellow lunch bucket with a peanut butter sandwich and a thermos of milk. When the bus came, the driver opened the folding yellow door and we clomped up the steps to where the O'Neil kids were already waiting for us. The rattling yellow school bus groaned into motion. It stopped again three miles later and waited for Alan Wilson and his brother Clive to get on—Clive was always late—and five miles further on it stopped again and we all got off at the Sirdar store. We crossed the highway, went down a narrow weedy path cut into the steep road bank, across the railway crossing between long lines of parked boxcars, past the empty station house, along the coal-dust laden road and into the school house.

Mrs. Hare was new that year as well. She had a school with seven grades, few resources and a motley mixture of students. In my grade one class there were three of us: Alan, myself and red-headed Santo Wood, whose mother was Dominic Pascuzzo's sister but who had married out of the clan to a red-headed Irishman. We started the day by singing The Lord's Prayer and O Canada. A picture of the Queen hung at the front of the classroom over the two blackboards and a row of geraniums with bright red flowers lined the windows.

Mrs. Hare came at 9 am and left at 3 pm. She always brought her small Spaniel dog with her. He lay in a basket all day beside her desk at the front of the room until it was time to leave.

The school bus arrived at the school at 8:15am and came back from town to pick us up at 4:15 pm. We had forty-five minutes in the morning, fifteen minutes at recess, an hour at noon and an hour after school unsupervised to do whatever we wanted.

Inside the classroom, Mrs. Hare kept strict discipline that she enforced with a yardstick. Outside was different; the biggest and oldest kid in Grade Seven gave the orders and decided what we would play. The rest of us followed along.

I was deeply excited by school. I organized my new pencils and my fountain pen, my bottle of ink and my wide-lined notebooks inside my desk at the front of the first row by the windows. We got workbooks in which to trace letters and readers with absurd stories about Dick and Jane and Sally and their dog Spot. Mrs. Hare believed firmly in phonics, which meant that we could learn words on our own by sounding them out. Once I figured this out, I worked at learning words. I discovered that learning a word was like opening a box within a box, only to find they were all connected together. Eventually I got very bored with Dick and Jane and their lives and discovered there was another shelf of books on the far wall by the Grade Sevens. I connected enough boxes to read a whole book–The Little Red Hen–that I laboriously sounded out, word by word until, with delight, I realized I understood the whole thing at once. I told my mother. I read it out loud to her. I felt like an explorer at the edge of a new land. There were books and books and more books and I could read them.

I don't remember what led me to believe from this that I could be a writer. But I do know I decided at six to be a writer and I never went back on the idea. It was always what I was going to do. In fact, I announced it to my family one night after dinner. What I don't understand is where the idea came from. As far as I know, no one in our family had ever met a writer or had any idea how anyone went about being such a thing. We were farmers or, at least, my father was and his father and his father before that; generation upon generation of Armstrongs who had been farmers and outlaws in Scotland and, when they came to Canada, married above themselves to women of gentleness and refinement and learning and then went on being farmers.

As school wore on that year I made other discoveries. We had a piano in the school and every day we would gather around the piano that no one ever played and Mrs. Hare would play songs to us on her creaky violin. We learned a lot of songs and that Christmas we had a concert. We practiced Christmas carols and the older kids had prepared a full three-act play about Robin Hood. My brother needed to be dressed in armour and my mother, in some puzzlement, wrapped tin foil around some old clothes, only to discover, to her deep chagrin, that Robin Cherbo's mother had made him a complete set of armour out of links of silver painted cardboard.

When it was time for the Christmas concert my parents, predictably, had a fight. Every event in our lives seemed to be occasion for a war. But finally, after everyone had a bath in the giant cast iron bathtub, we got dressed in our best clothes, got in the green Dodge pickup and drove to the school, where the playground that no one ever drove on was full of cars. The schoolhouse was jammed; people had driven from Creston and Wynndel and Boswell to come to our concert. Our program was an hour long, with two choirs, a play, some skits and a solo by Mrs. Hare on her violin. Finally Santa Claus arrived through the back door, which was never normally opened, and handed out candy canes to all of us. After that there was a table laden with the assortment of cookies, cakes, candy and other food brought by the mothers. My mother always brought delicious dyed-green shortbread Christmas trees that were eaten almost immediately.

We also produced a newspaper full of stories, poems and essays that we ran off on an old Gestetner machine Mrs. Hare carted out from town. Everyone had to contribute a story or a poem. Most of the kids hated this chore but I dove into it and took the task of writing essays seriously. In Grade Four I produced an essay on the balance of nature that was essentially a long argument with Wally Johnson, our trapper neighbour, who insisted that any animals beside birds and fish ought to be killed. My mother always complained about Wally. She said animals were all afraid of him because he smelled of death. Wally adored my mother and came to visit often. But my mother loved all animals and she hated trapping. She told me it was cruel and when she described it in graphic terms, I agreed with her. From then on, I argued with Wally even though I loved to listen to his stories. It was confusing because he was a lovable funny man who liked us and always brought us some kind of present, even if it was only the incredibly greasy doughtnuts made by his wife, Nettie.

It was from my mother I first heard the phrase, "the balance of nature." The rest I figured out for myself. I gave a copy of my piece to Wally, who took it very seriously and argued with me about it after that whenever he saw me. In the essay I wrote " Nature is a great and intricate puzzle...in nature, each thing needs another thing and man cannot do without any of them." My beliefs haven't changed much from this early awareness. I think I was so intense about this partly because I lived so intimately with our farm animals and read every animal book I could find—I identified with animals far more than I did with people—and because, instinctively, as almost all young children do, I had an inate sense of sympathy and care for nature.

Mrs. Hare and my mother ran together in my head and merged into one person. I got their names mixed up and routinely called each one by the other's name. Mrs. Hare let me stay in and read at recess and lunch hour. Our school was too small to have a library so, once she discovered my passion for books, she usually gave in to my request that I be the one to go to the elementary school in Creston and pick out a new batch of library books. And when I read my way through all the readers we had she let me sit with the older grades and read theirs until I finished them and then she left me to read on my own.

My mother had bought me *Black Beauty* for Christmas when I was seven. The book was written from the point of view of a horse, which made sense to me. After all, I understood horses better than people and I'd spent more time with them. From then on I read every horse and dog story I could find, although I was happy to read about almost any animal. I loved, for example, the Rudyard Kipling story about *Rikki Tikki Tavi*, the mongoose who kills a cobra, and read it over and over. After *Black Beauty* there was *Lassie Come Home* and, one of my all time favourite books, *The Yearling*, which I read and re-read and which my mother also read so we could talk about it. I still read it periodically and it is still good.

Since I was so hooked on animal books, all of the kids at Sirdar school ended up reading their way through *Lad, A Dog*, and the rest of the collie books by Albert Payson Terhune, which we all loved, and then the endless series of *The Black Stallion* books.

In the animal stories I read, the animals were always smart, powerful and good, while human beings, most of them, were treacherous or cruel or stupid. This only confirmed what I already understood about the adult world. But there were other books that also confirmed my view of the world that free and outside in the woods were the best places to be: *Annie Oakley, Robin Hood, Tom Sawyer* and *Huckleberry Finn*.

Adam Robertson, the principal from the elementary school in town, would come once or twice a year on a nominal inspection and, each time, he would call me up to stand beside the desk and read to him. Then he would go back to Creston and report back to the kids there that I was smarter than them. They hated me long before they ever met me.

Outside the long row of windows on the south side of the school was the flagpole, then a high mounded granite rock, surrounded by lilac bushes gone wild, which was variously a spaceship, a base for hide and seek, a police station or a ranch for the cowboys during cowboys and Indians.

In class we stared longingly out the windows, waiting for the life where we could become part of the brush, the woods and the granite hill to resume. There were also swings and a teeter-totter but those were dull compared to the games we could imagine. We lived our real lives, the intense and endless imaginary melodramas that began with someone saying, "Let's pretend," in and among and on top of the rocks, in the hollows beside the two enormous pine trees on the slope south of the school above the lake or in the tangles of brush, lilac bushes and wild apple trees around the school grounds. We played cowboys and Indians, cops and robbers, traveling in space. We made up names and characters and plots as we went along. When we did this, I entered into a kind of dream where the imaginary world was intensely real and sometimes coming out of it, because the bus was coming or it was time to go back in the school, was a shock.

There were two broken down old fruit trees and a crabapple growing over the cut bank to the north of the school. We hollowed out the dirt under the crabapple and made seats and from then on, when it got hot in May or June, Mrs. Hare let us move the school out under the crabapple tree.

The one place we were never supposed to go was the lake just below the school, a swampy reedy expanse of water called Duck Lake. No one seemed to mind or care about the water tower but over and over again Mrs. Hare warned us about the lake. In the winter, gas under the ice made hidden holes through which we could all fall and then, we were warned, we would disappear forever under the ice.

At home, Kootenay Lake was the place where I spent all my spare time. It didn't seem right to be going to a school on another lake and not go to it. One day I talked everyone into sneaking down through the thick willow and buckbrush, though the small meadow that marked the boundary of the allowable school territory, onto the skinny trail under the huge pines and then past the quaky aspens onto the long stretch of sand and rocks.

Duck Lake was different than Kootenay Lake. It was shallow and reedy, full of insects and fish and ducks. Fascinated, I stared into the brown water in which things swam and scuttled and disappeared out of sight.

Someone told on us and, since it had been my idea, for once I got in trouble with Mrs. Hare. I was her smart girl, her star pupil and for her to be angry with me was far more devastating than for my mother to be angry. The only other time Mrs. Hare had been angry with me was when, in Grade One, I figured out that the two times table and adding the same two numbers together got the same result. I wrote it out on the blackboard to show her but she sent me outside and told me I couldn't know that yet.

Our playground rules were oddly rigid. The toughest big kids generally decided what the games would be. When we tired of Let's Pretend, we played endless, fiercely democratic games of Scrub baseball, or we played Prisoner's Base, which involved drawing a line in the sand and daring each other to cross it in order to steal a pile of sticks. Sometimes we tied each other up and once we played a game of torture that gave me shivery weird feelings when I thought about it at night. Once I had started thinking about it I couldn't stop and I wanted to ask my mother about it but I thought she would be angry.

The brush around the school was a thick tangle of red willow and buckbrush. Only very determined small children, crawling on their hands and knees, molding the brush into tunnels, walls and rooms could get through it. We made rooms in the brush and nests out of long dried grass in the rooms. We piled up ammunition made from the tiny green crab apples and then we went to war with the apples that we whipped at each other with the long shoots broken off the apple trees. Alliances shifted, were made in an instant and then broken almost as fast. Life in the school was organized and, in its own way, interesting, but life outside the school was what called us to be fierce, dramatic and as brave as we could be.

One noon hour we gathered around the abandoned wooden water tower that sat just beside our playground. Some of the older

Chapter Four

boys had pried the boards off the wall and made a space into which we could crawl. Inside it was cool and damp and smelled of earth.

"Climb the ladder," someone hissed in my ear. "Double dare you."

I couldn't see anything in the dark. I inched my way forward until I held the rungs of the ladder in each hand. I began to climb and then I stopped. I clung to the ladder with both hands. I was afraid to move. I imagined the ladder rungs breaking underneath me, imagined myself falling away into the darkness. But I had to move. There were voices far below hissing at me but I had no idea what they were saying; there was light above me from cracks in the roof. Finally I climbed upwards with the abandon of desperation until I could crawl out on the small ledge at the top.

I could hear wings in the blackness; something brushed by my head. Swallows and disturbed bats wheeled and circled in the small fragments of light sifting between the broken boards on the roof. I sat there until I felt myself come back from the terrible place fear had taken me and then I had to slide back down the long blackness, hanging on and feeling with my feet.

When I made it back outside into the bright prayer of the spring sun, they were all staring at me. "Don't tell," hissed the older kids. "Don't tell or you'll be in so much trouble."

On another afternoon we gathered around the ancient rusted railway turntable. Once, when Sirdar had been an important railway depot, this turntable had been used to turn the railway engines around. The turntable weighed nine tons, according to my father. Someone had broken the lock off. We began to push. Someone got a pole and we levered and pushed and sweated until we actually got it moving and turned it all the way around. On other days we got up on top of the long lines of ranked boxcars and ran along them, jumping from boxcar to boxcar.

When Mrs. Hare came outside and rang the bell we came dutifully in the white door, past the pink tiles inside the girls washroom and the brown tiles inside the boys, hung our coats on the row of coat hangers and sat in our assigned seats, ranked by class, one row for each class. At the front of the class were two blackboards and Mrs. Hare's desk, under which her dog slept its days away. Alan, Santo and I started at the windows in Grade One and by Grade Seven we had moved all the way over to the far wall. One class at a time, Mrs. Hare would call us to sit at the reddish-brown skinny table at the side of the room, by the piano, to do reading or arithmetic. The black upright piano stood in the corner on far wall and, past that, were the sink and the hot plate where, everyday, we made soup for lunch.

Just before lunch hour one student was delegated to leave the school, to walk across the tracks and up the hill to Charlie Nelson's store to get a can of soup. Charlie Nelson was an old white haired man. He always wore a worn grey sweater that bulged over his huge belly and he had a sickly wife we never saw, who lived upstairs over the store.

One day it was my turn. The store was one of my favourite places. Every day after school we would play at the school until Charlie Nelson rang the bell and then we ran back across the railway tracks, up a narrow path and across the highway to the store because the school bus was coming. On Fridays my mother would give each of her kids ten cents. For ten cents I could buy a bag of potato chips or a chocolate bar or an ice cream or ten round bubblegum, which we got one a time from the bubblegum machine on the counter, or a lollipop. The choice was agonizing.

At the back of the store was a huge pile of ancient *Star Weeklys*, which I was determined to read my way through. The *Star Weekly* was a kind of glossy insert in the Western Prairie Producer newspaper and each issue contained a chapter of a romantic story for which I could never find every episode. There were wooden shelves piled with dusty clothes that no one ever looked at and glass cases full of ancient fishing lures.

Chapter Four

This day, when I came in the store, I asked politely for the canned soup, handed over my twenty-five cents and turned to go. Charlie Nelson grabbed me from behind and pulled me onto his knee. "Give me a kiss," he said. He fumbled towards me with his blubbery lips, his whiskery-white cheeks.

I pushed him away as hard as I could and ran out of the store and all the way back to the school. I didn't say anything to anyone. I hadn't understood what had just happened. It stayed in my head like a weird nightmare until, gradually, it wore away. But after that, I was also careful never to be alone with him and I never again offered to go for soup.

Now that I could read, I discovered books in our house, an odd and weirdly varied assortment of leftovers from previous generations which I found on rainy afternoons by scrounging through the boxes that had been left in the dusty crawl space over the stairs. There was a set of stories of Norse mythology, which I loved, and a Girl's Own Annual from England which had somehow migrated to our attic. I didn't understand a lot of what the girls in the story were saying or doing but that didn't matter. I think I was in my forties before I realized that a jumper was a sweater and not a pullover kind of dress.

My parents spent money on books, at least my mother did. My father once bought us a set of Science Made Simple books which none of us read despite his complaining. I tried but they were dull. I read my way steadily through everything else the house had to offer, even through all the Reader's Digest condensed books which my parents subscribed to.

For me, books were addicting. I read on my bed when I was sent upstairs to clean my room. I sat on the edge of the bed and thumped my feet on the floor to make it sound like I was working, until my mother crept up the stairs and caught me. I read under the covers with a flashlight. I read sitting upstairs, shivering in my cold room when I was supposed to be doing homework.

Somehow the books I needed and wanted to read showed up, although I still can't figure out how or from where. I suspect my mother had a hand in it without saying anything, but there were small miracles, one after another: *Anne of Green Gables, Treasure Island, Little Women, Tarzan, Robinson Crusoe. Robin Hood* in particular became an iconic book for me. Robin Hood lived in the woods, he was free of restrictions and duties; not only that but he was heroic and tough. And then I discovered another hero. Annie Oakley was the heroine of a television series at the time but we didn't have television. Someone gave me a copy of one of the Annie Oakley series of books. Annie was also young and single and free, she had a horse and a dog and a gun, which, to me, seemed to be all any girl would ever need.

My mother must have blessed the day she discovered something called the Open Shelf Library. This was a brilliant but short-lived idea where kids could order books from the Open Shelf Library in Victoria, for free, through the Post Office. Of course, it was a hell of a chore; first ordering the catalogues, then mailing the lists, then finally receiving the books and then remembering to pack them up and ship them off again. But it was all worth it when after school, I'd go to the Post Office and there would be one of those brown paper wrapped packages.

But it still wasn't enough.

We had a neighbour named Mrs. Arnold. She had been the teacher at the one room school in Sirdar. She had retired the year before I started school, so I never knew her as a teacher, only as my mother's friend.

My mother usually had one friend that she could talk to, but seldom more than one and, because of the farm and the endless work, she didn't visit anyone often. There wasn't an organized social life on

Chapter Four

the east shore and, even if there had been, my father wouldn't have wasted the time and gas money to go anywhere. So my mother made do with visits from relatives, usually my father's sisters, who she didn't like, or her mother, who came once a year and fought with my father; and when we went to town we had to visit my grandfather, who lived alone in a dusty small house that stank of must and mold.

We also visited often with the Wilsons and them with us. We went to their house for Christmas dinner and they came to our house on occasional evenings when the adults played cards and, on those evenings, no matter what the weather, the kids all got sent outside. Usually we played our favourite game, hide and seek. Occasionally we played softball and one year we invented an odd sort of golf, played with sticks and a torn softball over the rumpled garden and in and out of the piles of rusting machinery. And one of the greatest attractions, for me, was Alan's immense collection of comic books that he kept in a box under his bed.

My mother talked to Marg Arnold about many things and she mentioned my need for books. Mrs. Arnold had belonged to the Book of the Month Club since it had started. Every month, she bought whatever book was offered and put it on her shelf. One of the walls in her small grey house by the lake was lined with books. I don't know if she read them. Their dust covers were undisturbed and each one still had a bookmark from Book of the Month club describing the contents.

My mother suggested I go for tea on Sunday afternoon and bring back some books. One Sunday I walked the mile of gravel highway between our houses, along the twisting S curve up toward the O'Neil's house, past the place where Twin Bays creek muttered over its collection of sand and logs and down Twin Bays road, over the little log bridge and up the thin lane past the blackberry bushes, to her house.

When I came she always made tea. She had obviously baked for my coming and brought out plates of cookies which I impolitely devoured while we made conversation about the weather and my mother. We must have talked about other things, perhaps the neighbours or the scenery, but she told me nothing about her life and I never asked. I waited patiently for the moment when she suggested perhaps I would like to pick out some books and then I went into the chilly dusty living room, where it was obvious no one ever went anymore, turned on the single dim light and perused the shelves with the avidity of an addict being offered drugs. I picked out a stack of books and she never questioned my selection or suggested any choices. Even I knew some of the books were beyond me but it didn't matter, they were words and therefore worth something.

Once I had the books I was eager to go but she was less willing to let me. I stood in her kitchen, shifting from foot to foot, while she kept making conversation and I made little lunges for the door until at last I managed to say good-bye, managed to point out that it was getting dark and my mother would be worried (what did I care if my mother worried) and then I hurried back across the bridge, up the hill and down the highway through the close wintry dusk hugging my parcel of books to myself.

When Marg Arnold died I was in high school. I had long since ceased my visits. Many things had changed.

Marg had begun to phone my mother; we had phones now, black boxes that hung on the wall, that had party lines with individual rings for each house but, when you answered the phone, you heard click, click, click down the line as other people picked up and listened in. That was one of the things that had changed. Marg didn't drive much anymore and Mom and Dad had taken to buying her groceries or taking her to town with them on town days, which they didn't like doing because she was so slow. One day she phoned to complain that someone was on her roof, trying to get in her house. My father went up but of course, there was no one there. These phone calls went on for several weeks and, finally, my father got fed up. When he went to see her she was weak and sick and he persuaded her to go to the hospital. He and my mother had talked about it; it was obvious she couldn't go on living by herself—she had no family.

Now for the first time, my mother told me the little of Marg's story that she knew; she had a little girl, my mother told me, who died of pneumonia when she was four. Marg had never gotten over her child's death and had come here to bury her hurt and her sorrow. She lived in our small isolated community as a housekeeper to a dreadful cranky man named Jim Purcell and eked out a living as a schoolteacher until she retired. Jim finally died and left her alone to live in a house that didn't belong to her. After she died, it would go to Jim's son in the US.

She lived for a few days in the hospital. All she wanted to do was go home again and my father, none too gently, told her she couldn't. But my mother told me all Marg wanted was to die and see her daughter again.

After she died, the dreadful son came from Texas, driving a new Cadillac car. He clearly was irritated and uninterested in this chore of dealing with his father's stuff. He roared about complaining, told us Canada was full of Communists, put the place up for sale, sold everything and disappeared again. But the books came to me and also a picture I still have of Marg Arnold, young and beautiful and smiling, with her small daughter sitting in her lap. And every time I look at it, I feel both guilty and grateful.

Chapter Five

As I GREW OLDER, my life began to fragment into rigid divisions: work versus freedom; loyalty to my father versus protection for my mother; my grandmother versus the O'Neils; inside and outside; books and the forest. But I also had the land telling me I belonged to this place. This sense of belonging was my key to survival but I didn't know that as a child. All I could do was follow my heart and my gut to the places where I couldn't be hurt. I sat on the school bus in the morning, pressed my cheek against the cold glass and watched phantom wild horses flow past through the trees.

The farmhouse reeked of smoke and dust and ghosts. My mother cleaned and painted and wallpapered but still Pete's ghost snuck through the house at night, slamming doors or opening them again. The house was painted dark green and two Douglas-fir towered over the front of the house. When the wind blew, the trees swung and roared and I would go out into the overgrown front garden and listen. The front garden was enclosed by an unpainted picket fence. In early summer, a row of delphiniums in the deepest shade of royal blue towered over the lawn. They made a tunnel into which I could crawl, looking out through a fringe of blue upon the shadowed world.

Beyond the delphiniums to the north, through the fence, was a swampy piece of ground covered in ancient currant and gooseberry bushes, intertwined and overgrown with thistles and sweet clover. My brother Bill and I made tunnels here as well; ponds in the stream we could dam up and enlarge enough so we could sail wooden boats around in them.

In the front, under the walnut tree, the gate opened onto the dirt road; the first summer, my mother set out a table and a chair and my oldest brother and I sold bags of cherries to the few tourists who stopped and paid us ten cents a pound for a paper bag of cherries. My father got us out of bed at 5 am to pick cherries. He set the twelve-foot ladders under the tall branches and we scrambled up into the centre of the trees, twenty feet high, with buckets hooked to our belts, and scrambled back down with the buckets that weighed twenty pounds each when they were full of cherries. We ate cherries steadily all day and then had no appetite for dinner.

In the back yard was an old log woodshed full of strange bits of harness and tools and, beyond that, the log barn where every afternoon, Tiny the Jersey cow stood and bellowed at her calf, locked in the barn, until my father came out to let her in for milking and to let the calf have a chance to suck.

When I went out in the late afternoon to the gate by the barn, with my tin can of wheat, chickens came running from all over the farm. We had baby chicks now and they were my care as well. It was my favourite time of the day, standing by the barn gate, staring out over fields emerald in the evening light.

There was so much to see and explore, so many places that became whatever I wished them to be. In the pasture was a huge

Chapter Five

stone that turned into an elephant when I sat on its head. I had just read Rudyard Kipling's stories and I desperately wanted a real elephant but the stone stood in wonderfully.

Ranks of imaginary wild horses ranged the hills above me; at the beach the rocks sang to me in the exhausted afternoons after climbing down off the stinking headache making school bus and, among the rocks, golden-eyed fish that lived in their own kingdom sailed with majestic slowness through green-shadowed water.

In the summers, almost every evening I escaped to the lake. As evening fell I would sit on the Fishing Rock, watching the sun gracefully sinking down over the top of McGregor peak, gold light catching the forestry watchtower on its bald peak. A downdraft would start; I could hear it coming, sighing down the mountainside through the fir and pine branches.

Above me in the fields the dark was growing and the curlews were crying and crying through the shadows.

They're gone now. They've disappeared and I don't know why. My father says the ravens drove them away. But when I was a child, lying awake on hot nights, they cried and ran over the fields and I loved their cries more than any other sound.

I stayed at the beach until there was only a lingering rim of light behind the opaque blue mountains. The fish made circles on the water; the water slurped and lipped at the sand's edge like feet splashing, like something coming out of the black depths to visit. After it got dark the noises of the lake changed and became menacing.

There is a monster in the lake. Many people have seen it. On very hot summer evenings, our father sometimes took us out in the boat into the middle of the lake to swim. He would swim under the boat and grab our legs. He and our mother would talk about all the bodies that had been lost in the lake, the bodies that never came to the surface, the black endless depths of the lake.

But still I wouldn't want to go home. The fields were full of dark. The hay stubble would bite my bare feet. My mother might be calling. Mosquitoes began to haunt the air; light still glimmered in dim layers on the mountains. But I didn't want to go, not yet, not quite yet. The wind would come stronger now, enough to rock the trees, wake ripples on the water, which splashed with greater urgency—ghosts in the water.

The mountains were black now. Under the trees, up the path from the beach, I had to feel my way. The noise behind me from the water was menacing. I had escaped but it wanted me back. All day I had hovered by the water, staring into the green depths, looking for fish, caught in a dream of water and air, the sun tasting my skin, turning me to brown salt and leather. My skin would glow all night.

Floating back through the hay fields, half fish, half bird, blind across the bird-crying fields, with the wind and the black sighing trees and my mother waiting, calling me, singing, to come in, come in, come back inside.

The next spring after we moved to the farm, when I was about to turn seven, I came home one day from school and the two giant fir trees lay prone across the yard, across the fence, crushing the delphiniums. Dick O'Neil was there, sawing the trees into blocks with his chainsaw. The tree stumps were three feet through. I stopped in shock as I came through the gate. Then I did something horrifying. I began to cry. Those trees had been mysterious, enormous, giant friends that guarded the house. Something about their giant lengths across the ground, tree limbs severed and already piled for burning so the trunks looked naked and helpless. I flung my lunch case to the ground and ran to my mother, who would understand.

"They had to come down," she said. "They weren't safe."

I flung myself out of the house, out of the back door, across the pasture to the elephant rock where I sat with my head on my knees, staring at the mountains until it got dark.

Chapter Five

When I finally came in the house, dinner was almost done. The light from the kitchen shot into my sore eyes. Everyone sitting at the dinner table stared at me; my two brothers, my sister and my parents. I slid into my chair and my mother dished me potatoes and fried chicken and peas. I ate my food without raising my eyes.

"Don't know what the hell you're so upset about," my father said. "Just a couple of trees."

"They had to go," my mother said, more gently.

Words slogged in hopeless circles in my head. They were beautiful. I liked them. Nothing made sense. I knew for the first time that my father and mother were both wrong. I did the only thing I could. I finished my supper in silence and went up to my room.

One afternoon, after lunch, before I could escape, my mother said, "Come and help me."

My parents had been arguing all through lunch. My mother wanted to order new linoleum from the Sears catalogue and father said no, it was a waste of money.

After lunch she left the dishes sitting and went into the living room. Then she went downstairs to the basement and then came back up with a claw hammer. She shoved the old worn couch away from the wall and attacked the linoleum with the claw hammer, pulling it up in chunks and fragments.

"Come and help me," she screamed. Her voice went up and up like a machine revving up. Her hair was hanging in her eyes and her face was red. I stood in the doorway.

"Hurry up," she said. "You have to help."

This was not my mother, this harsh screaming stranger. Who was it that had let the dishes stand and was now screaming and pounding at the linoleum? I rather liked the blue linoleum. It had a border of flowers around the edge but now it was coming up in long ragged strips.

I grabbed hold of a strip and pulled. It came away with a satisfying tear, leaving patches of glue and grey underlay on the floor. There were rough boards under the linoleum. I knelt beside my mother and pried at the edges of the linoleum with my fingernails. My mother leaned back on her heels and wiped her hair out of her eyes.

"Should I leave your father?" she said.

I stared at her.

"Where could we go?" she said. "I used to be a hairdresser. I could do that again. Or I could work in a store."

I thought hard and fast. I knew my mother was always unhappy but the thought of her actually leaving was inconceivable. I thought about the farm, my parent's fighting and the endless angry voices at night until I fell asleep. I thought about being away from my father. I thought about leaving the farm and going away into a world I knew nothing about.

"No," I said finally. "I don't think you should go."

"I could manage," she said. "I used to work in a store. Or I could get a job as a hairdresser." She was crying now. "We never have any money. I haven't bought any new clothes since we got married."

"But we have the farm. And the animals. And our house."

What would happen to the chickens, I thought, without me to feed them?

"It will get better," I said earnestly. "I'll help you."

We went back to tearing up the linoleum and carrying it out onto the front lawn. When my father came in at four for tea, the linoleum was gone, lying in a pile of strips outside on the lawn, and the dishes were done. For once my father was speechless.

I never heard anything more about the linoleum. A few weeks later I came home from school and my father was running a rented sander up the down the rough boards in the living room. He painted them with varnish after they were sanded.

Chapter Five

My mother ordered a rug from Sears catalogue and every few weeks she would roll up the rug, coat the boards with hard wax, put the opera, *Aida*, on the stereo and give us pairs of our father's work socks to pull on over our shoes. Then we would slide up and down the wax until it was smoothed and buffed, shiny and slick as ice.

For a few brief years during the war, when my mother had her own job and her own money, she spent most of her salary on singing lessons. Now, somehow, she kept music in her life. She saved small bits of money and subscribed to the Metropolitan Opera Record Club; whenever she could afford it, she bought a new opera. The first few records she ordered were simple operas that we could all listen to and understand. I sat with the lyrics to *The Tales of Hoffman* on my lap and learned the melody and the lyrics. After my mother played an opera, she and I would sing it together. When Mrs. Hare asked us to memorize a song and sing it at school, I sang an aria from *Tales of Hoffman*. Mrs. Hare was astonished enough to phone my mother.

On rainy afternoons she would put on *Aida* or *Carmen* so we could all march around the living room and play at bullfights and then she got *La Bohéme* and, soon after, *Madame Butterfly*. I couldn't understand the words but my mother told me the story and the music itself was so desperately beautiful it was right at the farthest edge of unbearable. But still it was irresistibly, endlessly singable. Whenever she played music my mother would tell stories to go with it, about her days in Vancouver taking singing lessons, about her handsome singing teacher who had wanted to take her to Toronto, about how she had quit singing to marry our father, about how different her life could have been.

She sang at her work, sang to call us inside, pure operatic soprano notes floating over the orchard and down the hill to the water where we were hiding, escaping the endless work. My mother sang in her toil from morning to night, through the endless effort of running a farm and feeding everyone on it and producing everything from scratch. All our food came from the farm: meat, fruit, vegetables, milk and butter. Every fall 300 jars of fruit and vegetables lined the shelves in the cellar.

My mother had small hands. There were always sores breaking open on her hands; burns from the oven or cuts from a knife. Her hands were always so busy; even in those rare moments when she sat down she was knitting something, usually a sweater for one of us. The skin on the back of her hands was thin and delicate and the blue veins showed through. She kept her nails carefully filed but she seldom used nail polish.

"You stay in and help with supper," my mother said one afternoon. I barely glanced at her. I was watching out the window. Nora and Shirley would be by soon. Every afternoon they went to fetch their cows and horses home from the pasture south of our house. I went with them; either riding double bareback, if they were riding, or skipping beside them if they were on foot.

"You stay here," my mother said. "You're always running off with those girls. Stay home and help your own family."

"But I have to go," I said. "They're expecting me." I stared at her. I couldn't figure out why she was being so horrible. Stay in and cook? Instead of running through the woods, rounding up the cows and loping the mile or so behind them back to the log corral at the O'Neil's, a long stick in my hand? It was no contest.

"You stay inside," my mother said. "It's time you learned something about cooking. It's time you started to help out around here." Her voice rose and her face twisted. She grabbed a stick of kindling from the box beside the stove and smacked me with it. It stung but what stung even more was my mother's betrayal. She had been proud of my independence, my freedom.

Besides, she was being unfair and we both knew it. I worked hard; it was just that whatever I did was outside with my father. I

Chapter Five

loved farm work. I hated housework.

"I'm going with the O'Neil's," I said. "I hate this house. I hate being inside."

We faced each other. "Do what you're told," she said. She was yelling now, screeching, about the work and how tired she was. My mother was almost always warm and kind and understanding. She was the person I came to for defense against my father; she always understood and backed me up.

Snuffling and furious, not from the beating but from her inexplicable betrayal, I helped set the table and mash the potatoes, turned everything into bowls and called my father for dinner from the basement where he usually had several things that needed some kind of fixing.

I sat through dinner with my head down. I ate my food, because if I hadn't my father would have made me sit there all evening until it was gone, then excused myself and slid out the back door, through the pasture gate and into the field to one of my favourite hiding places, the hollow behind the juniper trees next to the orchard fence. I sat there through the gathering dark, planning how to run away and determined to stay out all night. But when the dark was fully descended, thoughts of bears and cougars intruded and I snuck back to the house, in through the back door and up to my room.

My mother was never really strong or really well. She was made for an easier life—and yet she had four children and a farm. My father was impatient with illness or weakness and, in fact, simply got frantic whenever my mother, or any of us, got sick. A sick cow he could shoot, a broken tractor he could fix, but a sick person had to be goaded and ranted at so we would get back to work.

"Work it off," he would bellow at his sick children. "Get outside and work up a sweat. That'll cure you."

When my oldest brother developed hayfever and came in from

the barn coughing and wheezing, our father told us all how he had been allergic to pollen and dust but had cured himself by working on a haying crew where most of the hay consisted of ragweed. A day spent coughing and sneezing in a haze of yellow ragweed pollen had cured him. The same treatment never worked for my brother but my father never excused him from haying work.

I came home once from rounding up cows on horseback with the O'Neil kids with my scalp torn open from a low-hanging branch. My mother demanded we drive the twenty miles to the hospital. My father was furious at the idea of wasting gas and time over something so trivial. But my mother won, for once, and a doctor used nine stitches to close the cut.

But my mother couldn't always work it off. She developed rheumatic fever soon after we moved to the farm but went on working, against the advice of her doctor, dragging herself through the days. It affected her heart and she took medication for it the rest of her life. But I didn't know this. I didn't know about her weakness, her exhaustion or her swollen and painful hands. I only wanted to be outside, in the blue twilight, running alongside the O'Neil's.

After the O'Neil's left, the woods were lonely. I trudged up the trails on foot where we had ridden together. I dreamed about riding, I woke in the morning, frustrated, from dreams of riding horses, so vivid I couldn't believe they hadn't been, in some way, real. So I began dreaming awake. I rode imaginary horses over the pasture and through the orchard to the beach, talking out loud to them. In the old machine shop at the back of our house, I lined up a series of sticks with twine tied around them. I printed out their names, the most beautiful names I could think of, and stuck them on the wall with tacks: Princess Beauty, Steeldust, Coaly-black. I had a horse of every colour. In a schoolbook I made up elaborate family connections for them. By this time I was reading every horse book I could get my

Chapter Five

hands on, so I had some idea how horses were named, that they had mothers and fathers and histories. I lay awake, dreaming of their names and their colours. They were so real to me that sometimes, when I ran to the machine shop in the morning, I stopped, surprised by the row of sticks tied to the wall by bits of twine. It required a trick of the imagination to get myself back into the world where these sticks were transformed into proud horses and myself into the princess-warrior riding them into various vague battles.

My parents didn't have the time or money to pay a lot of attention to their children's obsessions. But I was so obsessed by the idea of getting my own horse, they actually got worried. My father complained that horses were useless and ate too much. I didn't listen. I didn't care what he said. I ate and slept and dreamed horses and, over and over again, I begged for a horse of my own.

So they bought me a horse for my ninth birthday. The last time I had a horse to ride was when we kept two of the O'Neil horses for a summer. My father took me to see her before he bought her. He asked me what I thought. I had no idea what I thought. I only knew she was a horse, a brown horse, a horse that, if I said yes, would be my horse. So I said yes.

What he bought, for the enormous sum of $150, was a barely-broken, untrained, muddy-brown, three-year-old mare. When my father hauled her home in the back of the Dodge pickup and turned her loose in the pasture, she headed for the farthest corner and refused to have anything to do with any of us.

What we didn't know, and found out much later, is that she had been "broken," as the term went, when someone had stuck a halter on her head, beaten her half senseless, stuck a bridle and bit on her, ridden her around a bit, and pronounced her ready to sell.

I followed her around for weeks, with bits of apple and oats pilfered from the cows and chickens. I asked my father for advice and he grunted that she was my horse and if I didn't want her, she could go back where she came from. After a while, she let me scratch her neck and shoulders and one day, when she was lying in the sun, I lay down with my head on her round warm belly and we dozed together.

Even horses get lonely. One day Lady (which was the name she had come with) came to me when I crossed the pasture. She put her head in my arms and sighed the deep sigh horses make when they relax.

I went back to the barn and lifted the heavy old leather halter off the nail in the corner above the manger. I went back out. Lady was still standing where I had left her. I lifted the halter up and she stuck her nose in it. I did up the heavy metal buckle.

Then I tied a rope to the ring at the bottom and led her through the gate. I tied her to a tree and went and got a brush. I spent much of the rest of the afternoon brushing her and feeding her apples while she stood with her head down, half asleep. Finally I got the ancient bridle that had come with her and stuck the cold bit in her mouth and wrestled the earpiece over her ears. Then I slid on her back and rode around the house, down the lane, through the orchard and back up to the house. Before I turned her loose, I rubbed my hair all over her hair so I could sleep all night smelling that wonderful salty sweaty horse smell.

That night at dinner, I announced that I had taken Lady for a ride. No one seemed to think this was remarkable. What to me had been a miracle was passed over between the potatoes and the creamed corn. That night I took my horse-stinky hair to bed and lay all night in a stupour of happiness, dreaming of the places that Lady and I would go. And we did go, up and down the mountain, over the trails that the O'Neil girls had shown me. My father had given me a twenty-two rifle. He handed it to me one day, showed me how to load it, showed me where the shells were kept and said, " Learn to shoot it."

I had an Annie Oakley cowboy hat and a red vest. In the summer I galloped through the cluster of cabins full of gaping town kids. I rode up and down the highway, proud and tall, on my horse. I had a horse and a gun, just like Annie.

But Lady soon showed a genius for getting herself, and me, into trouble. She began to figure out how to untie gates, ropes, latches and barn doors. She got into the feed bin and ate herself sick; she tore down a whole line of white sheets that my mother had hung on the line to dry and trampled them into the mud.

When I woke in the morning, Lady would be tied to a tree in the yard. So I knew she had done something. It was always bad. It always cost something. One night she ruined a whole wagon-load of apples by leisurely chewing small bites of out of a few apples in each box. One night, the Greyhound bus driver knocked on our door. At the last moment, he had seen a black shadow on the road and screeched to a halt. Lady was stretched out on the warm pavement, sound asleep.

I began to tie her in the barn with the door closed. To get out, she had to untie a rope that I had knotted and double knotted, undo the latch on the barn door and then undo the gate. Somehow she managed it. Finally my father looped a heavy chain over the barnyard gate and wired it shut. This seemed to work.

My father thought that everything on the farm should have a job, should be put to work. Lady had no job, no use that he could see, except to starve the cows by eating all their grass; finally he hit on the idea that we might be useful driving the cows on their annual spring trip across the river, where they were left for the summer to graze. We brought them back again every year just before Christmas.

To get the cows to the river, we drove them five miles south along the highway to the railway bridge. My father went ahead in the truck and my brothers and I ran behind. The cows hated this trip and broke away at every opportunity, into the neighbour's yards, up old logging roads onto the mountains. They stopped traffic and stood stupidly in the middle of the road staring at the cars, while equally stupid furious drivers honked and waved their arms.

We ran and ran, while our father banged on the door of the truck and yelled instructions. Occasionally, when there was nowhere for the cows to go, we caught a brief breath on the running boards of the truck. When we got to the river, we banged on the rumps of the cows with sticks and rocks until, reluctantly, they crawled into the river and swam across. Then we could pile in the warm cab of the truck and go home.

Every year, we brought them back again just before Christmas. But first we had to find them. They were scattered through the marshy willow thickets at the south end of the lake.

We walked across the railway trestle, stepping over the black, creosoted ties, looking down at the dark green water below. The wind always blew through the trestle girders, viciously trying to snatch us off and throw us into the water. Then it was a three-mile march out to the other end of the dike, to Kootenay Landing, where sternwheeler boats had once tied up and received passengers before the railway track was built.

The cows were always hiding somewhere, reluctant to get moving, wary of people after seven or eight months on their own. We had to run through the swamp, through murky black water and mud, leaping from clump to clump of tall peppermint-smelling swamp grass, while the cows sloshed ahead of us.

After we got them across the river again, we ran behind them, all the way home. I once figured out that we had run, almost without pausing, for over eight miles.

My father thought Lady should be able to help with this, but Lady had figured out pretty quickly that she didn't have to do much of anything she didn't want to do. One thing she didn't want to do was be ordered around by me. Slopping around the farm was one thing. That was okay. She let me ride her; she stumbled and dragged

Chapter Five

her feet and slouched along and stopped whenever she saw something that might be good to eat. I tried riding her with a stick, the way the O'Neil's had taught me, but that made her shake and sweat and shy at everything so I fell off as much as I rode her. But running along the highway after a bunch of cows wasn't her idea of fun. She shied at every car, and because I didn't have a saddle, I usually fell off. We weren't much good as cowboys.

My father began turning Lady loose to run with the cows. I had to go and get her myself. After that, when winter came, I went and found her and rode her home alone through the snow, clinging to her back over five miles of snowy road, keeping my hands from freezing by letting go the reins and putting my hands up under the heavy hair of her mane on her warm neck.

The dream and my determination wore out. I rode her less and less. There weren't many places to go really and there were more and more cars on the road that had now been paved. And my father now used her as a kind of generic threat. Whenever he thought I had done something wrong, he threatened to sell her. He went on and on about her being an expense, a nuisance, a greedy useless waste of time and money.

There was only one way out. One day I said, "Fine, sell her then."

He did. Some people came, a nice enough couple, and then my father told me to ride Lady to Wynndel, where the couple would meet me with a truck.

Wynndel was twelve miles away. We had never gone on such a long ride. We rode there on a June morning and for once Lady behaved and didn't shy. We rode past the wild roses and the swamp full of red and yellow-winged blackbirds, past Sirdar where I went to school, up the long hill and eventually to Wynndel. I slid off Lady's sweaty brown-dappled back and handed the reins to the couple. I didn't look at her. I didn't say goodbye. I slumped into the seat of my father's truck and we rode home in silence. I never went out to the pasture if I could avoid it and I tried to stop dreaming at night about riding wild horses and escaping. But I never could. Night after night I woke from dreams in which I had almost gotten on a horse, almost gone riding, and then I woke up, bereft and lonely, in my white room with the rug made from my grandfather's favourite sorrel mare on the floor.

Chapter Six

FOR THREE SEASONS at the farm, school, chores and weekends bound our lives. But summers were different; in summer, we belonged entirely to the farm and, in fact, rarely left it. Time in summer wove in and out of contradiction; to our father, it was a desperate race to get all the work done. To us, summers were full of frantic work but they were also full of timeless hours at the beach, especially the long evenings on the rocky point where we headed each evening as soon as supper was done.

My father had organized the farm into an amazing place of subsistence where everything worked together. None of it made much money but it fed us and our animals and bits of money trickled in from here and there. A subsistence farm is an amazing closed system that works extremely well if there are enough people around to do the work. Most of our food came from the farm: meat, milk, butter, cheese, vegetables and fruit. About the only thing we didn't grow was wheat for flour although, for a while, my father bought wheat in bulk and ground it. What we never had was enough money. My father usually worked out at some part-time job, such as hauling lumber for the sawmill and, in summer, money came from selling cherries and raspberries to tourists from our fruit stand beside the road.

We had a small herd of cows, a milk cow, usually a couple of pigs, as well as chickens and sometimes geese and ducks. Our Jersey cow, Tiny, gave astonishing amounts of milk and cream. No matter how inventive our mother was, it was hard to get rid of three gallons of milk and two gallons of cream a day and most if it went to the pigs. We started eating out of the garden in June, when the strawberries and rhubarb and early spinach and peas were ready. Then we went on stuffing ourselves through the summer and into the fall; an endless abundance that we took for granted. We had a half acre of garden where we grew every possible kind of vegetable, plus we grew strawberries, raspberries, apples, plums pears, peaches, grapes, gooseberries and currants. My mother also made beer and wine.

One of our biggest chores was putting up hay to feed the cows through the winter. My father cut the hay with a cutter-bar mower he had adapted to pull with the tractor instead of with horses; all of the machinery on our farm was ancient and my father kept it running with a combination of ingenuity and adaptation. There was never money for parts so he made do or traded and scrounged for second-hand bits of machinery that could be adapted to fit. We had a Gibson tractor that was steered with a handle, a Farmall tractor that was a combination of several other Farmall tractors, and a Rumbley tractor that we hardly ever used. It had enormous steel cogs on its steel wheels; it could pull anything but it was huge and hard to start.

After the hay was cut, it dried in the sun for a day or so and then it had to be windrowed with a rake pulled behind the Farmall and then coiled into piles by hand. This all took a week or so and during this time, we all watched the sky. Rain would ruin the hay and turn it into moldy compost fit only for dumping. When the hay was finally dry we hoisted it into the hay wagon with pitchforks, drove it into

Chapter Six

the hay barn, lifted it out of the hay wagon with pitchforks into the barn, where it had to be stacked again and stomped down to fit under the roof. To build a proper pile of hay on the wagon required technique and care; I learned to stab the pitchfork straight down into the coil of hay, hoist it over my back straight into the air and bring it down flat onto the growing pile of hay on the wagon. When the stack was towering into the air and too high for us to reach anymore, we threw the last few forkfuls into the middle to tie it together. Bill and I climbed up and rode on the towering jiggling pile of hay while Phil ran ahead to open the gates. Once we got to the hay barn, my father heaved the hay up into the barn, forkful by forkful, while my brothers and I stabbed it with our pitchforks and tried to place it evenly into the corners of the barn. The first cut of hay in early July usually coincided with the worst of the mosquito season so we did all this in the middle of clouds of mosquitoes. We also did it in our bare feet. One day I was running behind the hay wagon on my way out to the orchard; I was behind because I had stopped to sneak a drink of lemonade in the house. I grabbed my pitchfork and started to run and then stopped. I stared down at my foot in astonishment. Somehow I had managed to stab the pitchfork right through my foot into the ground. All I could think of was how angry my father would be. I yanked it out and limped as fast as I could back out to the field.

The hay was cut twice each summer. We also cut hay in marshy meadows to the north of the farm at Twin Bays and in another meadow to the south of the farm.

Our other job was picking the cherries and raspberries. We had about thirty cherry trees that we picked from twelve-foot ladders or by climbing to the very top of the trees, balancing on slender brittle limbs, and stretching our hands to strip off every cherry. If we left any, our father made us climb back up and get them. We dumped the cherries from our buckets into wooden apple boxes, hauled them on the cart behind the tractor into the fruit stand, where whoever had been detailed for fruit stand duty weighed them out in five and ten and twenty pound bags and cardboard cartons.

Then there were the raspberries, seven long rows of them, which had to be picked every day or the raspberries would get overripe and fall on the ground. We got up at five to pick enough cherries to sell for the day and then, after breakfast, we started in on the raspberries, which we tried to finish by noon so we could go swimming. Every afternoon was a fierce and bitter negotiation over who got to go swimming and who had to stay and sell fruit to the tourists. We hated the tourists; there was no limit to the stupidity of their questions. They would ask things like, "Is this your farm? Are these your cherries? Can we pick a few ourselves?" Or they would quibble over paying ten cents a pound and demand to get a deal for buying a few more pounds.

By the time I was ten I was as strong as my older brother; I gloried in my own strength, in my ability to lift more hay, to climb higher, work faster, pick more cherries than anyone else. It was the only arena I had in which to excel and I competed fiercely to be as good as I could be.

My father's hands were huge, the skin thick as leather mitts. His hands were always littered with nicks and cuts, the lines embedded with grease and dirt. No matter how much he washed, they always had those black lines; they reeked of grease and motors.

I followed him everywhere. I had to stretch my legs to awkward lengths to match his strides. When he walked in the soft dirt of the newly plowed garden, I stretched hard to put my feet exactly in his footsteps, I stuck my hands in my pockets, grunted when someone asked me a question.

"You're just like your father," my mother would snap when she was really angry with me. It was true; I was my father's henchman and his enemies were my enemies. I believed in his raging endless

Chapter Six

despair about work and money, I followed behind him, snarling at my brothers and sister who wouldn't, or couldn't, work as hard, as fast, as well, as I could.

Once we were walking out to the hayfield in the spring. Wind came beating in off the lake. We were supposed to spend the morning picking up rocks, shards of granite from the outcrop that my father had blown up with dynamite. He liked to blow things up. I did too. I loved to help him. It's a miracle he never blew any of us up. He used to hand us sticks of dynamite, the paper damp from age and leaking nitroglycerine.

"Don't shake your fingers," he said. We put the dynamite down the holes he'd drilled with his ancient compressor, covered them with dirt and rocks and tamped the whole thing down with crowbars. He fixed the blasting caps, ran out the fuse, said, "Get down. Open your mouths."

That was to protect our ears. We all got headaches from the blast fumes and our crazy dog Willy ran in and began pawing at the blast holes even before all the rocks had stopped raining down from the sky. Maybe he figured the world's biggest gopher was down there somewhere.

On the way out to the hayfield my father began cursing my little brother who was lagging behind. I was eight, so my brother would have been five. My father was ranting about how we all had to work, when there was work to be done you goddamn well did it, that it was work or starve and, by God, we were going to work.

I saw it. I got it clear. It was one of those moments when life suddenly made sense. We were all in this together. We had this thing to do, called survival. I felt a clear and religious hatred. I hated my brother who didn't get it and was whining behind, scuffling his feet in the dirt and doing everything to get out of working.

Very occasionally our father stopped cursing the weather, the fruit trees, the contrary cows breaking through fences and getting out on the road. Sometimes he played, went fishing or took us all hiking up a remote creek across the lake to look for the rare and tender brook trout in the high rushing pools of Next Creek. In the summers we'd go on picnics and winters we went skating on the marshy spaces of Rat Slough, where he chased us with bulrushes breaking open in a foam of seeds.

One wintry day frozen sleet coated the hayfield and he took us out there in the old Dodge pickup and spun it in circles until we were dizzy with screaming.

I always felt safe with him, even reaching under the shrieking buzz saw to pull away lengths of wood or the time he knocked a tree over the power line. When the wires lay snaked and sparking in the grass he said, "Don't touch those," so my brother and I jumped over them instead.

And, although I never told anyone, I knew it was my fault the tree had taken out the power lines. He'd told us to push on it as he cut through with the power saw because it was leaning and the wind was blowing but, when I felt the tree lean its awful weight towards me, I weakened and let go. It bent over to squash me but I was too fast and ran out and away.

The farm belonged entirely to my father. He extended his fury at us, his lazy children, to his disobedient and wayward land. The rain rotted the cherries, lodged the hay so it couldn't be cut; weeds overran the pasture grass and the garden. One year the chickens got coccidiosis and died, all six hundred of them, and every day for a solid year we ate chicken, which my mother did her best to disguise as something else but never could.

I was terrified of my father and I worshipped him as well. He made the small kingdom that was the farm run; there was nothing he couldn't do, nothing he couldn't fix, nothing that, cursing and swearing, he couldn't manage, somehow, to deal with. Whenever he

Chapter Six

left, to go to work or to town, the farm felt different, as though a huge pressure had been relieved, for just a while. But we also knew that no matter how hard we had worked or what we had done, when he came home he would find something wrong, something to complain about.

But a war I didn't understand and couldn't win began between my father and me when I turned into a girl. Turning into a girl was a confusing process. For one thing, I loathed the whole idea of being a girl. Real girls had no fun; they stayed in the house and did housework. The few ordinary girls I knew from school were mostly silly. They weren't like me. They didn't know anything about the things I loved: farming, the woods and horses. They weren't tough. They cried instead of fighting.

I wanted to be a farmer and how could I be that if I was a girl?

But as I grew older, became more visibly female, more and more often my father sent me in the house to help my mother. I was supposed to be cooking and cleaning, doing laundry with the wringer washer, washing the milk cans, making butter and jam and canning things and baking; the work my mother did with barely a pause in her swift pace from morning to night.

When I was inside, I was the one to whom my mother complained. "How am I supposed to buy shoes for you kids?" she would worry out loud. Or, "How am I supposed to get you Christmas presents?"

When my mother got a worry, she would chew on it and then spit it at my father until both she and my father were exhausted. Most of the things she wanted my father thought were silly and a waste of money. I would go back and forth between them, trying to make peace. They sent me to each other with messages. Foolishly, I repeated these messages, trying to explain to each what the other one really meant. I always failed.

My father would respond, "You damn women, you all think alike."

And my mother said, "Oh, you're just like your father. You're always on his side."

I used to wonder which of them I could do without. I lay awake at night, upstairs in our creaking house, and imagined soldiers coming, giving me the choice. Whichever one stayed, the other would die a peculiar horrible death. I lay awake, imagining one choice or another, night after night. But I never did decide.

But now, as I spent more time with her, I was forced to begin to understand my mother. For the first time, as my mother and I talked, as we peeled fruit or mixed dough, I began to see her side.

I was the only ally she had. She didn't have women friends, didn't drive, rarely went anywhere without my father except occasional long bus rides to Vancouver to visit her own mother.

My mother was always there, in the house, in the kitchen. Every morning work stopped at eleven and everyone came in the house for tea or hot chocolate in the winter, or lemonade and cookies in the summer. And then at four the work stopped again and there was my mother, with fresh baking or a bowl of popcorn. She boiled the kettle, made tea, which we ate and drank and then ran out again while she got started on supper. She was just there, at the centre, and if the life of the farm had a soul, she was that soul, endlessly generating food, meals and comfort. And when we came in complaining about our father, or about each other, she took the side of whoever was doing the complaining, so that each one of us, smugly, jealously, assumed that our mother loved us the best.

I began to realize how much my mother wanted, not so much a different life, as more, so much more, of things she simply couldn't have: clothes and furniture and other small things for the house, for her kids. She wanted fun and joy and music and laughter. I promised my mother when I grew up and became a rich and famous writer, I would take her to the Metropolitan Opera in New York. It was the best thing I could think of.

Though now we sometimes sang together through the work, the work never stopped. She baked every day, at first on the wood stove and then on the electric stove that my father reluctantly bought, sometimes twice a day, cakes and bread and cookies. She made three full meals a day, porridge, eggs, toast and ham or bacon every morning, and lunch for my father. Every day my brothers and sister and I climbed down off the school bus to a house redolent with gingerbread or oatmeal cookies, with popcorn and hot chocolate. Then we scattered to do our chores while she made dinner. When all the pots and pans were on the stove, simmering and bubbling, she would sit in the old green rocking chair, under the lamp in the living room, put on her glasses and read something, usually the Reader's Digest, for fifteen or twenty minutes, until it was time to hoist herself up again and dish up the food.

The summer I turned twelve Dad got a job in Nelson, which meant he would be gone for the whole summer. All the work would fall on our shoulders. Somehow we did it; one night Phil and I worked until midnight getting in hay because we thought a storm was coming. The next day we were out raking the orchard hayfield to get in the last bits of hay; I was driving the Farmall tractor but I was half asleep. I saw that the tractor was heading for a tree but somehow I couldn't turn the wheel fast enough to stop it. I hit the tree and the front axle broke. This was a disaster and my father had to hurry home and spend the whole weekend, cursing and frantic, to get it fixed.

The next summer it was my mother's turn to be away visiting her mother. This meant that I had to do the farm work as well as the cooking and dishes. She was only gone a week but this was the week that my father decided to build a haystack in the Twin Bays swamp, a mile north of the farm. All through the hot and shiny day, the two of us threw hay onto the wagon, hauled it to the side of the field and built a mound of hay. The idea was that it should be square. I caught each bundle of hay my father threw up to me and tried to place it to grow a square stack. I stumbled and floundered through the growing pile of hay; the next day and the day after that we did it again until all the hay was piled in some kind of conical stack. My father covered it with a tarp and we left it. Just before we left he stood back, studied the pile.

"Looks like a damn corkscrew," he said. But I didn't care. I knew that I had kept up with him through three days of insanely hard work; I was almost as strong as he was, I thought. I could do almost anything he could.

But that fall, I began to panic. Although we started at Sirdar school as usual, within a month the school was closed and we were all moved into a larger school in Wynndel. Mrs. Hare was sick, we were told. And the year after that I would have to go to high school in Creston.

It finally dawned on me that I was going to grow up and become an adult like the ones I saw around me. And that meant by then I'd have to understand the world away from the farm well enough to function in it. It seemed an impossible task.

By now I had knobbly sore breasts growing on the front of me that I hated and tried to cover with bulky shirts. I'd begun to menstruate which I also hated. I had to wear pads that I kept in a drawer in my dresser. Everything about being a girl seemed stifling, messy or embarrassing.

I didn't know who to ask for advice. I couldn't ask my mother because she was the one who always asked me what she should do. Or, on the rare occasions when I did ask her what to do, she'd tell me

Chapter Six

some story about her life that had nothing at all to do with my life. When I was finally old enough to start resenting this, I decided she had got stuck somewhere in her own past, like a needle stuck on a record. Her stories were all about when she was a girl, that long ago and unimaginable time my siblings and I called "the olden days."

Of course the olden days weren't real. They were stories our mother told us sometimes after dinner to make us laugh, stories she had honed to a high art which left us shaking and helpless with laughter, stories which that couldn't possibly be true—how she and her best friend Louise stole a bunch of Indian horses one night and headed for the border and nearly made it, or how my mother's brother wouldn't go to the outhouse at night so he started peeing down the knothole in the back of his closet, and his mother couldn't figure out where the stain was coming from that spread in a great yellow blotch across the living room ceiling. She told us these stories over and over and we never got tired of them, because she continually invented new details that made them even funnier and more ludicrous and impossible than they had been the last time we heard them.

So, the summer I turned thirteen, I should have known better than to listen when my mother began telling me stories about the wonderful times she used to have with her friends and saying how much I needed a friend. The next thing I knew, she had invited someone named Janet to come and stay for the summer. I sort of knew Janet. Her parents had a summer cabin next to our farm and I saw her when we all went swimming together. A couple of times she had invited me back to her parents' cabin, which was lined with flattened beer cartons. Her father worked at the brewery in town and enjoyed a special status among the men because of his endless supply of beer.

Janet was as foreign to me as a Martian. She was from town, for one thing. Town was only twenty miles away, but I only went there four or five times a year. When I did, I gawked like a tourist at some foreign land. Most of the time my father drove to town by himself, bought what he thought we needed and came home again.

Town was a place of exotica. Town was a place where once or twice a year they'd show a Walt Disney movie and my mother would decide that we should go. She and my dad would fight about it for days before my two brothers, my little sister and I were finally bathed, dressed in our best clothes and loaded, four kids and two adults into the front seat of the Dodge pickup, for the long ride to town. When we got there, we ran ahead of them all the way to the movie theatre, which smelled of popcorn and excitement. Then of course, they argued about whether we could have any treats, an argument which my mother eventually won, and finally, hands dripping with ice cream and popcorn, we got to go into inside the theatre. The movie was always an anticlimax after that.

My mother's idea was that not only would Janet and I have "fun" together, we could also get even more work done. She would pay us all some money this summer, she told us, for our usual summer chore of picking raspberries and cherries and selling them to roadside tourists. But this didn't work out so well because Janet, who was fifteen, wasn't remotely interested in working. She had only two interests, boys and smoking, about which I knew nothing. The boys came first but the smoking was important. It was an integral part of her preoccupation with her clothes, her blonde hair and who she was going to marry.

One afternoon she insisted we cut pictures of our future homes out of old magazines and paste them in a scrapbook. I probably pasted two pictures before I lost interest and began reading my father's old True Magazines. These were full of stories of hunting and fishing, about which I actually knew something. But Janet filled up the whole scrapbook.

The problem was, there weren't any boys. There was my older

brother, who was too shy and out of it to count, and there was the occasional boy from the summer cabins next to our place. Maybe Janet had envisioned hordes of teenagers driving out from town to visit us. But she did what she could to liven things up. Occasionally, when she did find boys, we walked along the highway and smoked. Or we hid at the end of the raspberry rows and smoked. Or we all met in a cave near the beach and smoked.

Janet had this idea that we should fix up the cave as a cozy little place with cushions and a fireplace and who knows what else, so that we could meet more boys and smoke more cigarettes. I was half sick and dizzy all the time from the cigarettes. I agreed to everything.

By now she had actually found a boy, a totally forgettable monosyllabic male person who had some dim connection with my brother. But she had visions of a romantic meeting spot and, though it looked like a damp miserable cave to me, I went on nodding and smiling.

In fact, I did whatever Janet did. In no time at all I was her idiot twin, drooling and tittering in the background. I stretched my lips and giggled. Whoever I had been seemed to have disappeared, without a struggle. Actually that person was still there, far away, hating Janet and waiting desperately for her to leave. Which I knew she would, eventually. But in the meantime, the only thing that mattered was that Janet must have no idea of what an ignorant, untowny, nauseated-by-smoking person I really was.

This beach was a place where I had spent most of my time for many years, but the beach as I had known it vanished the second Janet set foot on it. None of the things I knew were of any use any more–how to build a fire from dry grass and wood shavings, or how my brothers and I used to race over the rocks and the long, thin tangles of driftwood logs laid between them. Or how I had once swum all the way to Red Man's Point across the bay and jumped off a rock twenty feet above the water—none of this counted or mattered. My world had fallen away. While she was there, I had to live in this new world that Janet had brought with her.

Janet went away at the end of the summer and never spoke to me again. The next year I started at the high school in town where she completely ignored me. There I went on pretending I knew what was going on and trying to behave like the other kids. It was the only way to survive. The trick, I soon decided, was to get better at it but that was much easier thought about than done.

My mother said, "Oh, you'll have so much fun, there will be so many new kids for you to get to know."

My mother had never gone to high school. She imagined it as an idyllic place where we would all be girlfriends together, giggling and talking about clothes. She imagined and hoped that her lonely daughter would now be surrounded by friends, would finally be a girl among girls.

What she and I didn't know is that the principal from the elementary school in town had been using me as a threat for years, telling the kids there that I was smarter than them. It was true; I got my picture in the paper every year for topping the local achievement exams. But my mother always said, "Oh, Mrs. Hare coaches you for those exams." Since neither my parents nor Mrs. Hare had ever made a fuss over this, to me it didn't seem important.

Our high school was carefully ranked along hierarchies of intelligence and class. I was in 8-A, a class full of girls who were the daughters of the town, the dentist's daughter, the newspaper publisher's daughter, the daughter of the owner of the local sawmill. They had known each other all their lives. They knew how to dress and what to say and what was permissible. They knew the rules. They knew that they were the smart and fashionable girls and that they deserved this. I knew nothing.

Chapter Six

I was too tall. I stooped over in a futile effort to look shorter. I was taller than anyone else, especially the boys. I didn't know anything about those girly essentials: hair, makeup and clothes. I had just gotten new glasses. I wore hand me down clothes from my mother. I wore the wrong shoes. Everything about me was wrong.

There is no worse experience on earth than being alone at noon hour in high school where everyone else is in a clump, a gaggle, where looks and giggles follow you down the hall, and where loneliness is a yellow poisonous fog, a panic in which you are forced to dwell.

At first I hid in the library where I could pretend to be studying and where no one else ever went voluntarily. There were a lot of books in the library, more than I'd ever seen before. I began to pull them down off the shelves almost at random, take them back to a table and read. Then I began to take them out. I read books that no one had ever taken out of the library.

I read travel books and books by strange philosophers and novels and stories. I didn't pay much attention to the writers. As far as I knew, writers were people who had once lived far away, usually in England and were now long dead.

As I cowered in the library, I made another discovery. There was a whole shelf of poetry books that some well-intentioned librarian had bought years before. I began to look at them and then I began to read. Then I took several of them home.

From then on, in all my classes, I sat at the back of the room with a book on my lap. My teachers, either out of charity or incompetence rarely bothered me. Algebra made such little sense to me I might as well have been looking at Egyptian hieroglyphics.

Instead, I was reading Dylan Thomas, T.S. Eliot, Robert Frost, Carl Sandburg. In Math and Science, I was deaf to the teacher, thrilling instead with the discovery that words could make such amazing music. Poetry ran into my veins like wine. It resounded in my head like drums and bugles. I went around with "Fern Hill" banging in my head for weeks, thinking I was crazy, thinking I was the only one who had ever felt this way.

The librarian at the front of the room behind the desk never looked at me. The only other kids in the library were boys serving detentions. They blew spitballs and wrote notes to each other.

But even discovering poetry and travel books about places I'd always wondered about didn't make up for the tramp of feet and shrieks of girlish laughter in the hallways that I could hear from beyond the library, where usually, at lunch hour, there was just me and the librarian. Even going to pee was an ordeal since because all the other girls went to the bathroom in clumps. Once inside the bathroom, they backcombed each other's hair, used up endless cans of hairspray and rolled the waistbands of their skirts so that the hems were just below their crotches.

It was the miniskirt, puffed hair, blackened raccoon-eyes era. Every night I slept uneasily on huge spiked rollers trying to get my hair to puff and, every morning, by the time the groaning orange bus had lumbered through town to the doors of the school, my hair had fallen again into limp dullness. I hiked up my skirt and braved the washroom and then went to the library.

Every day on the long way home on the school bus, from the high school in town, the big boys in the back yelled and farted and threw left over lunches and hit each other. Johnny Fajnor, our driver, kept his head down, his eyes on the road, no matter the craziness going on behind him. For the last five miles, the bus was mercifully empty except for my brothers and sister and me. We never talked to each other on the bus or at school. The hierarchy of seating on the bus was rigid and we never challenged it. The front was for little kids, the

Chapter Six

middle for older girls and the back for the big boys. Coming home we sat as usual, my sister up front, myself in the middle, my brothers at the back. When we stopped—our house was the last stop—I went in the house, drank several cups of scalding tea and then I changed my clothes and went outside, first to the lake and then up into the trees on the mountain above the house.

The journey into the trees was a miraculous passage. At the borderline, between the trees and the pasture, I hesitated, waited, and then tentatively stepped into the silence. The farther I went into the blanket of trees, the more invisible I became.

Inside the forest was the opposite of school, empty of noise or movement except for the squirrels announcing, call upon call, that I was there, a stranger in the woods. Sometimes the ravens followed me, silent except for the faint hiss of their wings, from treetop to treetop. Some days I found a place that seemed to be a room inside this castle of endless rooms. There, I sat on the ground like some miraculous fungus and tried not to think. I wasn't doing anything as fancy as meditating, which I had never heard of. Sometimes I asked myself what I was doing there but I had no answer. I was doing what I had to, being nothing. Doing nothing, being nothing, barely breathing.

Entering the forest was entering another world—a door closed behind me and an infinity of doors opened. The forest was all possibility—room after room of mystery and discovery—but what I wanted most was to be hidden and alone, coming into some other dwelling, with other hidden residents all around me, leaving deer tracks, bird calls, chewed cone remnants at the base of a huge yellow pine, scuff marks by a hole under a stump.

One day I got off the stinking yellow bus and drank my tea. Then I changed my school clothes, went outside and wandered across the pasture, through Sawdust Bay and up the hill, over the rocks, down through the mossy ravine, to the place where seepage gathered into a round pond in the forest. The water was black and the poplar trees around it were bright gold. I sat on the ground. A muskrat made a thin line in the water pointing at me. It came out of the water, patted itself dry with its hands, then walked toward me and crawled up on my shoe. It sat there on my shoe and looked around. It was round and brown with gold tints in its fir. It picked up a poplar leaf and stuffed it in its mouth bit by bit, chewing along the edges of the leaf until it was done. I could feel its thin warmth, its weight through my muddy sneaker. I tried not to breathe. Then very leisurely, it fussed at its fur, thoughtfully scratched an itch with one foot and waddled back into the water.

Coming home another evening, I stopped beside a porcupine who very nicely let me stroke its quills. I found there was one sandy hump above the lake where the coyote den was and, if I went quietly enough, the coyotes would sit there and watch me go by.

Sitting still, the only time markers were the wind breathing the trees, the little humming in my throat as I breathed.

In winter, I watched the rose-purple light fade to the faintest hint of blue along the edge of the mountains. I would wait until there was just enough light to see my way home and then I would get up, stiff from the cold, and I would half see, half feel my way down the mountain.

Once I was in the yard I would stand outside, watching through the yellow-lighted window at my distant near family, saying things I couldn't hear, moving around. Oblivious of me. I would think of the deer and ravens and the squirrels in their dark safety, in their bitterly sweet cold world and, finally, I would go inside. No one asked me where I went. I had no idea what my brother and sister did after school. I didn't want to know. I didn't want to know they existed. I only wanted to spend enough time in the silence; I needed to soak in enough to get me through the next day.

Chapter Six

The only other bright spot in my life was our Grade Eight homeroom teacher who was young, new and energetic. She was also our English teacher. She was the first person I had ever met who was interested in writing. She asked us to write stories and the first one I wrote was a long story that went on and on for pages. Once I got started writing, I couldn't seem to stop. When I brought it to school, my teacher asked me to read it out loud. The other kids stared at me, rolled their hair on their fingers, looked out the window. Or passed notes to each other.

And then one day, my lovely young English teacher decided to start a drama club. The first meeting was held in a small room at noon, which, fortunately, meant I could go. All the other school activities seemed to happen after school and, since I had no way to get home other than the school bus, I couldn't go.

The teacher handed out scripts for a play and asked us to read. Finally, something I knew how to do. I found myself cast for a lead part and the club began meeting almost every lunch hour to rehearse. The few other kids who also joined the Drama Club began to talk to me.

I no longer had to hide in the library at noon. I found a new home, even some new friends. My talent for mimicry and pretending finally had an outlet. With huge relief, I disappeared into the characters I played on stage as well as into the role of the school drama queen. I still didn't have a clump of sisterly bodies to hide in but I had a role and that was something.

In Grade Nine we performed Shakespeare's *Taming of the Shrew*. I was so excited by the idea of Shakespeare that I went home and memorized the entire play in less than a week. I loved Shakespeare. My mother had bought me a complete set of Shakespeare's plays the Christmas I turned twelve and I had read my way through all of them, no matter that I only understood a quarter of what I read.

I turned myself into Katherine, the lead character. I became loud and quarrelsome. I fought with everyone at home. One night I dyed my long hair bright red and, that night, I didn't bother to sleep on huge lumpy uncomfortable curlers. The next day I went to school with bright red, straight hair hanging down my back. All day, girls with puffy bee-hived sprayed hair snuck up to me and said, "I love your hair," but they said it with lowered voices, looking around to make sure no one else was listening.

One girl who I had, until then, only admired from a distance said wistfully but with some pride, "I wish I could wear my hair like yours but my boyfriend would kill me."

The play was a huge success. After the play was finished, I began secretly, carefully, writing poetry in my diary. I knew it wasn't very good poetry but I published some in our high school newspaper. I went on reading, trying to figure out what I was doing wrong and why my poetry didn't sound like that of Dylan Thomas or Carl Sandburg. One day our English teacher invited a local poet to talk to our class. He was a gentleman farmer from England who lived on a ranch a few miles from town and raised cattle. I didn't really understand his poetry but to me he was a revelation. He was a writer and he was alive and he lived in our community. We were invited to ask questions and my hand shot into the air and stayed there. No one else seemed very interested.

But I had learned something. There was poetry. There was the sound of drums and bugles. There was the sound of words marching on their way to accomplish some great thing, to bring new truth and beauty into a plain grey world.

Poetry was many things to me but it was most like music, a stark music, music made only with words and images, that sang over and over to me again while I skulked, miserable and hunched, down the corridors of the high school.

By now I was not only reading poetry. In Grade Nine I discovered philosophy. I had already asked my mother for a copy of the Bible, which she bought me one year for Christmas. I read my

Chapter Six

way through it and decided, regretfully, that Christianity wasn't for me. It didn't make enough sense, although it was interesting. And I was quite taken with Jesus and much of what he said. But I also discovered Nietzsche and Thoreau. In Math class, algebra and geometry were as understandable to me as Arabic, and I read Walden Pond instead. I caught my breath at its magic and stared out the window at the maple trees on the lawn of the school; here finally was someone, I thought, who knew about some of the things I knew, about woods and solitude and walking. I decided on the spot that not only was I going to be a writer but also a philosopher. I read now incessantly—I read on the bus all the way home so I always arrived at the farm dizzy and sick. I read late into the night and over the breakfast table in the morning. Sometimes, on the bus, I would lift my head out of my book and think as hard as I could about the universe. Someday, when I got time and I had read every book, I would figure it all out. It was hard to find philosophy books in the library. None of my teachers asked what I was reading. But the philosophy books I did manage to find filled me with such longing and excitement about a world I might someday belong to, that often I had to stop reading just to breathe and think.

But what I really knew about the outside world was almost nothing. We didn't have a television, although my parents always diligently and dutifully listened to CBC news at noon and during supper. So what I knew came from the radio and from books. Since most of what I read was nineteenth century English poetry, novels and philosophy, my view of life was somewhat skewed.

One day our English teacher said, in the course of some discussion, that she would never take that new drug, what was it called, LSD, because she was sure she would see snakes. She had a phobia about snakes, she said. I had no idea what she was talking about.

On Saturday mornings CBC radio played, for half an hour, something called rock and roll. My mother was scornful about rock and roll. She said it was nonsense; it wasn't real music. Real music was classical music. She particularly hated Elvis Presley. But she let me listen to this CBC program.

One morning, John Drainie, the host, said he was going to make an exception to his general rule to not play songs longer than three minutes. This was a song, he said, that he thought was going to be important, that was going to change the music scene. And then he played all twelve minutes of Bob Dylan singing "Like a Rolling Stone." It's odd to listen to things that you know are important but you don't know why. It's like listening to echoes of a distant explosion. I listened to the whole song and I knew there was another world that I had to find out about. I began to listen more closely to the news. I began to think there was another world I could belong to besides the farm. I nagged my mother into buying me a guitar, let my hair keep growing, began to wear black and practice folk songs in the privacy of my room. I took a little bit of summer fruit-picking money and ordered a transistor radio from the Sears catalogue. And from then on, I would lie in bed at night and listen to bits and snatches of music, like messages from a far away and unimaginably distant world.

But high school went on being miserable. I began to win prizes—I entered essay contests, public speaking contests. I won provincial awards for acting. But nothing I did made my classmates like me. Standing out was not the idea. Everything I won only made things worse.

The annual local beauty pageant was coming up. I looked at the rules. They gave each contestant money for clothes. I didn't hesitate and I didn't think about it. I needed new clothes to go off to university next fall. I entered the contest.

Chapter Six

One Saturday afternoon, the six other girls and myself met at the home of one of the local dancing teachers. She made us walk around with books on our head and step with our toes first and then our heels. We had to meet every Saturday afternoon until the beauty pageant. One afternoon, we were fitted with hideous flower-patterned suits with short tight skirts and matching pillbox hats that we had to wear whenever we made a 'public appearance'. My suit was too small and the hat kept falling off but when I said so, the dancing teaching stared at me and then looked away.

Every practice, every meeting, became an exercise in humiliation because I soon figured out that the contest was rigged; it wasn't about talent or looks, it was actually about selling raffle tickets. The girl who sold the most tickets, we were told, would win. I didn't know anyone, besides my family, who might want to buy raffle tickets.

I ordered my clothes from Eaton's catalogue; a green dress, a long pink frilly gown. The evening of the contest, the woman who was supposed to do my hair and makeup ignored me. One of the other women took pity on me and put my hair up. I got through the contest and the next day, I sat on the float in the annual parade in my new pink long frilly dress, and waved and waved, sick with nausea at how embarrassing the whole thing was. We were all supposed to walk around all afternoon in our dresses and represent the young ladies of the town. All I wanted to do was escape to the safety and anonymity of the woods.

Chapter Seven

IN THE FALL OF 1967 I went off to Vancouver for the second time in my life, this time to go to the University of British Columbia. I rode the Greyhound bus to Vancouver and I got a room in a rooming house. The first time had been when I was eight and had gone, briefly, to stay with my grandmother. All I had been interested in on that visit was getting a good supply of comic books. The city hadn't made any impression on me then. Now I looked at Vancouver and thought it was ugly—all straight lines and concrete walls. But it was a place I knew I had to try and understand.

I walked around UBC and went to my classes like a child who had found a golden castle in the sky and knew she could never belong. I hid in the library, where at least the books were friendly.

I was an odd and confused mixture of things. I knew I was smart, I could win contests, I could write and I knew that what I wanted most in life was to be a writer, and I knew that none of that really mattered. I wore my new clothes like a disguise, a mini-skirted polka-dotted green suit with an emerald green raincoat. But, even in disguise, I knew I didn't, couldn't ever really, belong at UBC.

And every time the bus went down Fourth Avenue, I stared out the window at the people living there, the people in beads and feathers and bright clothes, who spoke a language I wanted desperately to understand. They seemed like bright angel people who had fallen from the sky. They would never speak to someone as ordinary as me. But they were free, I thought, the way I had once been free, in secret, in the woods. I took classes in English and philosophy and history and anthropology. I went back and forth to the rooming house on the bus. At night, I ate dinner with the other student roomer in our landlady's gloomy shadowed dining room and then hid in my room and read.

The year before, in high school, I had started going out with one of the English teachers. He and I had met on one of the trips the Drama Club used to make to other schools. He was one of the chaperones. To my surprise, I had discovered I did have the ability to flirt. One night he pulled me into an empty classroom and kissed me. After that he began coming out to the farm on weekends. We went for long walks and held hands. My parents liked him. My mother pronounced him handsome and he and my father had long conversations about tractors. He liked kissing, which I found boring but put up with.

Now, in Vancouver, even though I wasn't at all sure I wanted to, we began spending evenings and then nights at his place. Sex seemed interesting at first, and it was certainly comforting, and desperately necessary, to have someone to be with in the confusing wilderness that was Vancouver.

I didn't know anything about sex or birth control. I read up on the rhythm method and hoped it would work. It didn't.

I spent a long afternoon in the UBC library looking up books on pregnancy and what to do about it. Then I called Brian. We went for coffee at restaurant down the street from the boarding house. He

Chapter Seven

immediately asked me to marry him and I refused. All my dreams—writing, university, independence were vanishing before my eyes.

We went on arguing about it over the next few weeks. I couldn't move, couldn't breathe, couldn't think. He kept pointing out how irresponsible I was being, how unable I was to care for a child. Finally we moved in together and, that spring, we got married at the Anglican church in Creston.

We got a small apartment in Kitsilano. Brian got up and went off to teach every day while I finished my first year at the university. I had dived into philosophy like a starving person and now I sat, staring out the window of our small apartment at the Vancouver rain, reading the existentialists. I read and read. I plowed my way through Sartre and Camus and Simone DeBeauvoir and then I turned to Aldous Huxley and Erich Fromm. Some days, when I stopped reading, it was hard to think of any reason to do anything.

Pretending came so easily by now. After all, I had practiced all through high school. Now I pretended as hard as I could to be married and normal. I cooked and cleaned Some days I took myself out for lunch while loneliness flowed around me like fog.

On my nineteenth birthday, I gave birth to twin daughters. Immediately after they were born, a starched looking nurse whisked them away to the nursery. I lay in the narrow white hospital bed with my stomach, that so recent ballooned with babies, now caved in. I curled up on my side, under the bright fluorescent lights, on scratchy white sheets, my brain a puddle of incoherence and finally, I fell asleep. I dreamed I was under a grey sky, on grey sand, beside a grey ocean. I was carrying my new twin daughters in my arms and I was desperately running away. I began to sink into the sand. I realized I had run into quicksand. I held the babies up as high as I could and then, as the sand began to cover my face, I threw my children, hard, at the people who had been following me, from whom I had been so frantically running away: my mother and my husband. I threw my children to them and then I sank into the sand and died. I woke up almost immediately, gasping for air, panic-stricken.

At some point, when I was a teenager, I decided I would never have children because I was going to be a writer. It seemed obvious to me that having children would not go with that ambition.

Besides, I knew nothing about children. My mother, stuck in the house, was trapped by work and poverty and caring for four children. I was determined not to replicate her life.

A couple of days after the birth, Brian and I brought our daughters home. We named them Dorothy and Avril, after their grandmothers. I put them in the cribs that he had prepared for them. I wrapped them up the way the nurses had showed me and then I stared at them. I was afraid of them. They were mysterious with their gasping gaping mouths, their random hands blindly seeking, and their eyes that looked everywhere and nowhere, that looked right through my pretensions and into my private heart

"All right," I said. "You can have me, all of me." I meant it.

The next day I started back to university while a kindly neighbour woman babysat.

A few days later, my mother and my grandmother came to visit. They seemed somewhat bewildered by my desire to keep going to school.

"Your life is over now," my grandmother said sternly. "You must live for your children."

Instead I went on being a student and a mother and, I hoped, eventually a writer. Most of the time, these roles seemed to me to be irreconcilable. Nor was it possible to give any of them up. Persistence, however difficult, seemed the only option. But such persistence made my life tense, frustrated and fraught with tension. Despite my vow, I was an inattentive and exasperated mother.

Chapter Seven

I practiced writing in the bits and pieces and cracks and fractures of my life; I learned to live there as well. I read there; books piled beside the bathtub and beside my bed. My husband slept beside me as I read. I took English, History and Philosophy and I read and read: poetry and novels—Canadian poetry, Canadian novels. Leonard Cohen has just started publishing and I fell in love with his work. I began, again, writing poetry in secret.

In 1968, UBC was a colourful and amazing place. Protests against the Vietnam war were an almost weekly occurrence. Jerry Rubin showed up to speak and the students took over the Faculty Club. Other students occupied the Dean's office or overran the Student Union building.

Whenever I went for lunch in the basement of the Old Auditorium, I stared in fascination and secret envy at the people in beads and feathers, in leather and Indian cotton. I tried smoking marijuana and, that whole night, I lay awake beside Brian, watching optical miracles of colour and patterns dance across my inner sight.

I got up in the mornings and struggled to cope with classes, two children, housework and cooking. I had never really learned to cook. I had helped my mother bake and can, but making three meals a day seemed an overwhelmingly complex challenge. Fortunately, I had an old copy of the Joy of Cooking. I read the whole thing one day and realized that cooking actually had logical principles behind it. Every day I painstakingly made dinner using a recipe from the Joy of Cooking. I cleaned, badly, and did the laundry and took the girls for walks. At University I took classes in English and History and then I hurried home again.

But I was bored and confused. None of this was a life I wanted. I loved my kids but I didn't want to be a mother and a housewife like the women who lived on either side of me. I wanted to be outside, I wanted some kind of freedom, even if I had no idea what that freedom looked like or what it could mean. I had no idea what I wanted. I just didn't want what I had. And I still wanted to write.

I began babysitting a neighbour's child. This neighbour, Miriam, was Jewish, blond, and had embraced 'hipness' with a fierce intensity. She had married an Israeli man whom she met on a kibbutz. Miriam's life was revelatory. She had grown up in Vancouver. She saw it as a vast playground where everything was accessible to her and the rules were made for other people. She shoplifted, her house was a wreck, she never bothered cooking, she did endless amounts of drugs, and she got straight A's in her classes at university. She lived her life with a kind of careless, carefree, fragmented elegance that made me feel stodgy and dull. She treated me like a kind of pet. I went to parties at her house and came home confused and completely dissatisfied with my dull life.

Consequently, a couple of years into this experience of marriage and parenthood, I realized if anything was going to change, I had to do something. I just didn't know what to do. I still didn't understand the city, or people, or how to survive on my own. I had never had a job, never had my own bank account, didn't have a driver's license, didn't have any friends beside Miriam, who wasn't so much a friend as someone who had collected me as a curiosity and soon let that drop.

But I also realized that being married was nothing like a bad friendship I could somehow slip away from.

Finally I told Brian, this very nice and kindly man, that I wanted to leave. I sat up in bed one night and said, "I want a divorce." He had no idea why and neither did I really. It was an act of pure desperation; and even I couldn't believe those words were coming out of my mouth when I said them.

He looked at me. He was hard working and respectable and loved his family. The established realities in our marriage were that he was older and I was younger, he had a job and I stayed home, he was sensible and I was an impractical dreamer.

Chapter Seven

I wanted to take back the words mostly because I couldn't figure out who had said them. They just hung there, shimmering and vibrating like some kind of evil spell, like that green globe in the Sleeping Beauty movie, one of those long ago Disney movies. I'd been waiting in some kind of terror for years for that glowing green globe to show up, hypnotize me, lead me up the stairs to the witch who would finally, gently, put me to sleep.

But now I wasn't going to sleep. I was waking up, into a place where I didn't know what to do next, although the situation clearly called for some action. It took several months to sort out but soon I was a single parent, going to school and taking care myself and my two daughters. Brian gave us enough support to get by on and he very kindly went on paying my tuition at UBC and coming by when I needed anything. He was bewildered and sad and I was guilt-stricken and angry.

The kids and I got by on our own for a while but it was hard work. I was hungry for experience, for people. I needed to grow up and understand what was going on around me. I was very lonely. After a while various people started to come came by to visit and I smoked a lot of drugs and had sex like everyone else because those two things were at least easily available.

One day I had a great revelation while sitting around being stoned and waiting for it to wear off so that I could figure out what to make for dinner. I was staring out the window of my house and I saw someone walk by dressed as a cowboy, complete with leather jacket, white hat and toy guns. I got it finally. Everyone was dressed up and pretending to be someone. That meant there wasn't any truth anywhere, not in human beings anyway. I just had to pretend better.

By now I was dressing in long skirts and had let my hair grow. I got a job for the summer; an odd little theatre company was founded by my ex-high school drama teacher using money provided by one of Trudeau's youth employment programs. I left the girls with my mother and began hitchhiking back and forth from the farm to Creston. One night a man in a cowboy hat, driving an new truck, picked me up. We went for dinner and then to the bar. I hated drinking because it scared me. I hated feeling out of control. But the cowboy-hatted man told me he was a scientist, studying bears in northern Idaho. He invited me to his cabin. "Bring the kids," he said, "I love kids."

The next day we drove around a rutted logging road, just across the border. There was a cabin set in a rolling meadow. There were several other younger people who were, he said, helping with the bear study.

There was booze and drugs and stories around the fire at night; it all seemed free and charming. When fall came, he went away as well. I went back to Vancouver, back to school. But school seemed foolish; I had almost no money. When Herb showed up in Vancouver, he seemed like a lifesaver. He bought the girls and I food, took us out, bought toys. Gradually I stopped going to university. I didn't withdraw, I just disappeared. Now Herb's story had changed; he was part of some underground resistance movement against the Vietnam War. He had been in South America. He had met Che Guevara. We had to keep moving. We left Vancouver and drove south across the US. We had a tent and some sleeping bags. Whenever he ran out of money, he phoned someone and more money appeared. We bought a Volkswagon bus and crossed back into Canada. We went to Montreal and then turned west. We picked up hitchhikers and shared drugs. Every night I made dinner for us all over a campfire.

That fall we rented a house north of the farm. He got a job in a local bar and got fired almost immediately for stealing. He got into a fist fight with my father. We lived on the cheque Brian sent me for child support and the food my mother gave us.

And I was pregnant again. My third child, Geronimo, was born in the Creston hospital on a snowy Christmas eve. There was no one in the hospital but a nurse. The doctor on call was at a party. Herb wandered the halls of the hospital looking for something to steal.

"The baby's coming." I told the nurse.

"You have to wait for the doctor," she said. But there was no waiting.

When the baby appeared she said, "It's a boy."

"His name is Geronimo," I said firmly. I had been reading about Apache Indians. They were my new models of toughness

When I came home from the hospital to our rented house a couple of days later, the counters and table were piled with dirty dishes. People had showed up for a party while I wasn't there. I cleaned up and went to bed. Herb went out drinking.

I nursed the baby and fed the girls and grew a garden to try and feed us all. I knew there was something terribly wrong with this relationship; not just the drinking, nothing else was making sense either.

One day while Herb was gone, I began to search. I looked through his clothes, his suitcase, his few belongings. Finally, I looked under the seat of the car. There was a folder of papers, not much but enough to tell me things I hadn't known before. He had a prior wife, he had two other sons, he wasn't from Texas, as he had said, but from Washington.

When he came home, I confronted him. He left. I spent the next few days alternately furious and then scared. Somehow, even though Geronimo was only three months old, I was pregnant again. I had nowhere to go. My parents would take me in but I couldn't face this final humiliation, this admission of what an utter, complete and bamboozled fool I had been.

I hid it all. I took him back. That fall we left for Arkansas, where his family lived, in an old truck. We left my parents a note.

The problem was, Herb was not only a consummate liar, he was a charming and charismatic liar. He was a person who had made up his life and saw no reason why a made-up life couldn't be quite satisfactory, and even more fun than a real one. Mostly, in order to do this, he stayed drunk. Booze made living a pretend life a lot of fun.

We made it to Arkansas a long harsh drive later, and he introduced me to his family, his real family. The first question anyone ever seemed to ask me in Little Rock was what church I went to. The second was whether I wanted a Coke. Herb's mother, Hassie May, even had her own church, some hillbilly evangelical offshoot. Hassie May paid the down payment on a ramshackle white house on a corner.

The girls started school. They had to walk several blocks by themselves. They were two of the only white faces in the school. "Don't talk to anyone." I said. 'Come straight home." One day they were late and I panicked. I called the school. The kids were all still locked inside while the police shot it out with some man who had robbed a Safeway clerk and then locked himself in a house next to the school. The police shot the house and the man to pieces while the kids watched out the windows.

Naiches was born in a southern charity hospital. After he was born and I was taken up to the ward, I asked to see him.

"No ma'am," said the nurse. "We don't let the babies out of the nursery for twenty-four hours."

'But I want to nurse him," I said.

She looked at me as if I had just spoken Martian. I got up, got dressed, found the nursery and demanded my baby. Everyone shook their heads. I was obviously hysterical. I should go back to bed. I wouldn't.

Finally a woman sidled up to me. "I'm the dietitian," she said. "You're right. Get your baby and get out of here. They can't hold you here."

Finally they brought me papers to sign and I picked up my baby, called a cab and went home.

Chapter Seven

My children ran and played while solitude wrapped its fragile wily tendrils around me. I sat wrapped in a blanket on the couch and watched the pattern of leaf-shadows on the ceiling. I began to read again. I got a library card from the university library. I took a course in Creative Writing. I bought books from second hand stores and piled them in bridges and walls around the couch. In the evening I sat on the porch alone while the children ran through the dusk. At night I sat in a rocking chair, nursing the baby and dreaming.

The South was a place utterly foreign and peculiar, where people seemed to mostly go to church, drink a lot of Coke and hate people of a different colour. Everyone I met asked me what church I went to. The summers were unbearable, hot, wet, stifling. We had no air-conditioning. Some days I could barely move.

In the long hot afternoons, I lay on the bed in the ramshackle white house where eight of us were living—me, four children, my unemployed husband and his two unemployed grown sons from a previous marriage—and I discovered that if I held very still with my eyes closed and remembered every detail, every smell, the colour and texture of each rock, the feel of the sand, the blue silky water, the sough of wind, the damp, fishy, green smell under the shadow of the cliffs, I could almost get back to the beach at the farm. The beach lit up in my head like a searchlight.

A year later I was still sitting in the dark in that small white house in that boiling hot and ugly city. After a loud and terrible fight with Herb, I had slammed the door behind him and all the glass had fallen out in pieces on the floor. We had no money. The fight had been about him getting fired for being drunk. It was over. I knew that, finally. Now I had to figure out how to escape.

My parent sent me some money and I hid it in the lining of my coat. I made friends with one of the neighbours and, because I didn't know her and might never see her again, I didn't mind telling her the truth of what my life had become.

She helped the kids and I run, one evening when Herb was out drinking. We packed a few things in a bag and she drove me to the bus station. And after a long, bedraggled, grueling three day bus ride, there I was, back at the farm, back home, with four kids hanging on to my long skirt. We slept upstairs in my old bedroom for a couple of weeks and then I slumped reluctantly into the welfare office in Creston, surrounded by kids.

Welfare is an interesting system. It's there to catch you if you fall, as long as you have fallen long and hard so you have nothing left and you must crawl in there, suitably bedraggled, skinny and repentant.

When I came into her office, the social worker looked at me with suspicion.

"What did you do with your husband?" she asked, as if he were a piece of luggage I had misplaced.

I tried to bite down the various flippant answers that rose to mind. I hadn't eaten or slept much for weeks. In fact, friends told me later that I looked like a refugee from a camp somewhere, skinny, exhausted and dressed in clothes that I had worn to rags over the last couple of weeks. But I was proud of the cheque she finally, begrudgingly, handed over. It was at least a version of standing on my own. For the first time, I felt that I owned my life.

I bought a 28-foot trailer from a neighbour, with money I borrowed from my parents, and the neighbour brought it down on a flat bed truck and placed it across the yard and around a bend in the driveway from my parent's house.

The first night after we moved into the trailer, I sat alone in the dark. I'd bought groceries and clothes and shoes for the kids with the welfare cheque. The kids were all asleep in their bunks. I put on some music I'd borrowed from Mom, Tchaikovsky's *Winter Nights*. I curled up alone in the close and holy, music-washed, dark. I was home again. I could finally stop pretending. It was 1974. I had been away from home for six years. Now, two husbands and four kids later, I

Chapter Seven

was back, utterly bewildered by it all and totally ashamed of my new status as a welfare mother. I had been the smart one, the one my mother depended on, the one who was going to save her and take her away to New York, to the Metropolitan Opera.

After a while I began to look around to see who else was living nearby. My childhood friend Alan Wilson had also dropped out of university and come home to take over the family stonemason business. He had married someone I had known in high school and they also had a child, Jess, the same age as my youngest son Nat.

Alan and I had gotten the highest marks in our graduating class in the Provincial entrance exams. I came first and he came second. But, after his first year of university, he had left, gone to Europe and now he was back home, working in his father's business. I began spending a lot of time visiting with him and Joanna.

My mother soon found her consolation for her disappointment, in her grandchildren. They adored her and spent a lot more time at her house than they did in the trailer. She said to me, "Don't think I'm going to be your baby sitter."

And she never was. She never had to be. The kids were always at her house anyway. We all went back and forth from the trailer to Mom's kitchen many times a day. When he was two, Nat used to get out of bed first thing in the morning, pull on a hat and run across the yard, barefooted and bare-bummed, to Grandma's house, where she would feed him hot chocolate and toast fingers with strawberry jam. When I would arrive in search of him, he'd be sitting up in her bed, propped on several pillows, grinning triumphantly at me.

At night, I would sit in the trailer and stare glumly out the window, watching for grizzly bears, UFOs or my drunken ex-husband who had phoned with threats to come and kidnap the kids and kill me. I sat with the poker on my lap and listened to sad Linda Ronstadt songs, unwilling, unable to lie down and go to sleep. I went back to reading and writing; I started a book of poems and I started writing a novel and short stories. I had left University a few months short of my BA. Now I wondered desperately if I would ever get back to that impossible golden city and find a way to fit in and prove I belonged.

And then Herb, a man I thought I had safely left behind in the southern US, did show up. Now here he was, with a car full of presents, swearing he had quit drinking, swearing he had straightened out his life. All he wanted, he said, was to visit the boys, to be supportive, to give us money and buy the boys new clothes. I let him drive out of the yard with them and a couple of hours later I knew he wasn't coming back. I called the police, I called lawyers and then I borrowed some more money from my father and got on the Greyhound bus for a three-day trip to the southern US city where his mother lived.

I sat on the bus in an ancient fur coat that my grandmother had given me. I stared out the window as the land rolled past. My sense of myself as a person with a home, a past, a future, dwindled and disappeared. I didn't eat or sleep, but sat and stared and waited and tried to plan for the unknowable.

Staring out the window in the middle of the night, I thought I heard the land beyond the windows speaking. "You're still at home here," it said. "You can be home anywhere on the earth. You will be all right anywhere. Your home always goes with you."

I held on to that.

I made it to the city and phoned and his mother and her husband came to get me. They took me to her house where my children and my ex-husband were staying. I gathered the boys in my arms and wept. I promised to be a good wife and mother. I pulled out every dramatic trick I had. I begged to be allowed to stay; I had changed my mind, I said. I said I would become a Christian if that's what they wanted.

They didn't believe me. They arranged for members of the family to watch me. They searched my clothes and purse but they didn't find the wad of money I had stashed in the lining of the fur coat.

Chapter Seven

Finally someone made a mistake and left me alone with the boys. I grabbed my coat and purse, put one boy on each hip and ran to the corner where there was a city bus stop. I took the bus downtown to a motel and the next morning I took a taxi to the airport and got on the first plane that was leaving town. It flew to Chicago. I got off the plane in Chicago and took a cab to the bus station. I had enough money left to buy a ticket to Butte, Montana. I called my parents collect and they agreed to meet me there. The trip would take two days. I had $10 left for food.

I sat in the roped off section of the bus station that was marked for women and children only and I prayed to whatever powers I could think of that might listen. Tall black men prowled the walkways and corridors beyond this section. The boys wouldn't stay put. When they finally fell asleep, there was a bomb scare and the bus station was evacuated. I tried to pick up both sleeping boys at once and a woman I didn't know intervened and offered to help.

"Where are you from?" she said, and I made up a name and a story that she didn't believe. But it didn't matter. She gave me some money and I thanked her and thought perhaps I could make the money last by just feeding the boys. We made it to Butte; my parents picked me up, we drove back to the farm and I thought perhaps now my life could finally begin again.

But not quite. I was pregnant again. A month later I left my children with my mother yet again and got on a bus and went to Vancouver. It took a week. First I had to go before a three-man board of doctors and swear that having another child would endanger my mental health. Then I had the abortion. I wanted this child. I wanted all my children. But I had run into a wall I couldn't get past. I had so little left in me, so little strength and energy and what I had, I wanted for my other children. And so I let this unknown person go.

I took the bus home. I sat up wide-awake for the twelve-hour trip. The sun was coming up as we came over the Selkirk Mountains, over the Kootenay Pass, and down into the Creston valley. The sun stained the snowy mountains orange and pink and salmon. The trees were black beside the road. I leaned my head against the cold window. All I wanted was to be home, taking care my children and keeping them safe, but I knew I had to do more than that. I had to somehow, make a new life, both for myself and for them.

My mother in Vancouver, with two friends. She was working in the Boeing Aircraft factory and taking singing lessons.

The farmhouse built by Pierre Longueval, bought by my grandfather, William Armstrong, in 1938.

My mother with myself and Alan Wilson as babies on the Mannerino Farm.

My father at twenty. This is his school picture during the year he spent at the Olds Agricultural Institute.

My father and I at the Mannerino farm

In Riondel, at the bunkhouse

An evening in summer at the Riondel beach, Dad, Phil, myself and Bill

For years most of our income came from selling fruit to tourists. This was our first attempt, the summer we moved to the farm.

My brother Phil and I on the O'Neil horses, Gypsy and Lady.

My mother with Robin, Bill and myself sitting on the Rumbley tractor

My mother with her German shepherd dog, Farah.

My mother in her new log house, finally finished in 1991.

The old farmhouse.

The beach at the farm, looking north.

Chapter Eight

THE SEVENTIES WERE A COLOURFUL, intense and interesting time in the Kootenays. A new movement of strange but determined pioneers had arrived. They came in groups, usually, and they came with dreams although most of them didn't come for long. But they completely changed the small sleepy backwoods communities of the Kootenays by their presence.

There have always been waves of people wandering into the Kootenays, looking around, maybe finding something to exploit, maybe not, and then that wave has always receded, leaving behind a detritus of mine tailings, stumps and dams, or log houses and rusting machinery slowly being swallowed by thimbleberry and alder saplings.

These new people were following a long line of people who had headed into these same hills, looking for some kind of mystical metaphysical freedom and found it, only to find that they too had to live with neighbours who often didn't share their idealism, their ideals or their approach to the land around them. There were the

Quakers in Argenta, the Doukhobours in Castlegar and the Slocan, and the Mormon polygamists in Creston.

Although every place attracted its share of dreamers, the Kootenays have always attracted more than others. People have always perceived it as a place of cheap land, clean water, forested wilderness, empty blue valleys. People have come for land, for freedom to pursue their own individualistic lifestyles. They have tended to follow the same pattern set by the first European settlers: find a patch of available land somewhere on the mountainside, cut down trees, build a house, make a patch of garden.

Now, in the early seventies, everyone suddenly seemed to have the same idea. People went 'back to the land' in droves. There was a craze for all things rural. Rural life somehow suddenly seemed freer, healthier and more attractive than an urban life. It was an odd boom and didn't last but, while it did, one of the main places the new settlers came were the Kootenays. They left the cities of both Canada and the United States in Volkswagen vans and old milk trucks and ancient school buses and trucks with painted campers. They came, and for a brief while the country was a colourful place. People talked in wonder about chickens, about log houses, about yurts and teepees and solar heated greenhouses. Everyone was reading the new magazines that had sprung up to serve this trend—such as the *Mother Earth News* out of the United States. At every party dire warnings were repeated, with an odd undertone of anticipation, about the imminent crash of the outside world. And often it did seem as if the social order was on the verge of collapse. The media was full of warnings about the demise of the nuclear family and hullabaloo about the younger generation going to hell. The environmental movement, the women's movement and the peace movement were gaining strength. It was a hopeful time, when some segments of North American society seemed on the verge of inventing new ways to live.

But despite their visions of hippie rural life, the new people discovered that rural life is, in fact, often enormously complex and difficult. Everything costs, either in money or labour or time, and it certainly isn't free socially either. People discovered, sometimes to their horror, sometimes to their relief, that their neighbours and, in fact, the whole community were watching every step they made and commenting gleefully to each other about each new hippie folly.

The new people were often draft dodgers from the Vietnam era draft or deserters from the American army. They had visions of communes and ideas for new societies; many of them had money with which to buy land, build their houses and try out their dreams of community. At one point there were five communal settlements in the Slocan Valley and who knows how many more up and down the roads of that previously secluded quiet valley that had been settled primarily by Doukhobour people, miners and loggers. On the east shore of Kootenay Lake there were no actual communes, but people rented old houses in which a varying population of residents came and went. Or they lived in half-built cabins or tents or tipis or unfinished overly ambitious houses. In theory, living a life close to the land, growing your own food, being part of a close rural community all looked possible, but the one question no one seems to have asked was how they were going to support this idealistic lifestyle.

There is only one way to make money out of raw land and that's to exploit what it has to offer: trees, water for power, land for growing crops, minerals, fur, fish and meat. The newcomers of the seventies were coming to a land that they perceived as wilderness, but it took a while for them to perceive that it was in fact already under siege from people who wanted something from it, and that something was generally meant to serve the needs of the booming metropolis on the west coast.

The rivers had dams on them, the mountains had been logged once and were being logged again—huge clear cuts and roads spreading up every mountain valley. Although the era of mining and railroads had gone, the era of roads up every valley and along every stream had just begun. People kept finding little patches of soil to grow crops on—but the good soil, what there was of it, had long since turned into orchards or grain fields or hay fields or cattle pasture.

It was a land that looked wild but wasn't. Still, people held on to the idea that this was a kind of wild utopia, where you could live out your ideals and be who you wanted to be, even if it was never as easy or mystical as it first appeared.

As the new neighbours moved in, most of them discovered the farm and came for vegetables or advice or information. My father was running a backhoe business and he kept coming home with stories of the strange people he had been asked to work for. That first spring, after the kids and had I arrived at the farm, I had planted an enormous garden to make extra money. I also decided to supplement my welfare cheque by picking and selling cherries, as I had done all those years as a kid. I got to meet most of the new neighbours this way.

One day an ancient black Ford pickup rattled into the yard. Everyone in the truck spoke French or German except for one little girl who informed me gravely that it was her birthday and that her family needed some vegetables. They came every few days after that. My parents did their best to cope with this onslaught of new neighbours. No one who came to the farm ever left without something: a gift of apples, fresh vegetables, a bottle of homemade wine.

Patti, my brother's ex-girlfriend, lived just to the north of us in Marg Arnold's old house. She would pull into the yard every morning on her way to work, usually out of gas or in some kind of jam. Patti was tall, with red hair and lots of energy. She couldn't stay put. She told me she usually moved every couple of months but she managed to settle down at Marg Arnold's old white house on the beach in Twin Bays for a couple of years. She worked as a waitress in Creston and drove a succession of ancient cars. When I was with her and we pulled up to the gas station, she would call out to the attendant, "Give me a gallon of gas and a quart of the heaviest oil you got." She chain-smoked and my father always gave her hell for it. Her daughter, Tammy, and my two daughters quickly became inseparable.

"Guess what happened," she'd start, whenever she showed up. "Just guess what happened now?"

We never could. Her stories were always wonderfully on the edge of unbelievable. One winter morning she got up and, in turning around, backed her car over the blackberry bushes and into Twin Bays Creek. Her horse ran away and was hiding on the mountain somewhere. Or her dog had attacked someone's sheep or chickens again, and she was hiding it from her wrathful neighbours.

Summers in the Kootenays often include a lot of rain. On rainy July days, when the garden was too soggy to weed, the cherry crop splitting from too much rain and then rotting in the damp, the lake too cold for swimming, mosquitoes hiding sullenly under the trees and brush, we would all drift into Mom's kitchen. Inevitably, Patti's huge, red, fish-tailed Pontiac would squeal into the yard, spitting gravel as she swerved to avoid kids, bikes, dogs and cats.

Mom would bring out her latest batch of wine, "to taste," she said, just a taste, fussing and nervous, saying she really ought to let it age a little longer, but we could have a glass or maybe two. She made wine from dandelions or from birch sap that my father tapped in the early spring. She made wine from strawberries and raspberries and cherries and plums. There was always a new vat brewing behind the wood stove.

The kids got to try out the new batch of homemade root beer, bringing the brown bottles up from the dusty basement, where they mixed the foaming rootbeer with dollops of homemade vanilla ice-cream.

Sometimes other neighbours would arrive, drawn by the idleness the rain created. The talk would be slow at first. Patti usually had a story about the latest man she'd picked up and moved into the house, to do mannish things like chop wood and change light bulbs, and how he had then disappeared into the bar for a week without telling her where he was.

Dad would start to talk and Mom would interrupt and their voices would ramble into familiar rhythms. The dogs always snuck into the house with each new visitor and Dad would pause to snap, "Mick, get outside," and Mick would ignore him because he was Mom's dog. Instead he'd sneak under the table, where she fed him gingersnaps.

The rest of us would all talk at once, stories weaving in and out of the noise, several stories going at once, people joining in or dropping out. The kids would be somewhere and then someone would notice it had stopped raining and, suddenly, there was too much to do again, things to weed, transplant, pick, freeze, can, clean, mend, cook.

The sun usually came out by late afternoon. I'd drift out to the orchard to stare at the soggy trees and the musty drip-smelling earth, heat lightning grumbling away behind Castle Mountain and a purple thunder haze hanging sullenly in the crevice above Canyon Creek. I'd go back to work in the garden for a couple of hours and then I'd go down to the lake and wander along the rocks, beside the rain-glazed grey water. As the day faded into the long summer twilight, the mountains looked like a Japanese print, ranged one behind the other in dimming opaque shades of cobalt blue. Finally I'd come back home to the trailer, where the kids were watching our tiny black and white TV, their minds mesmerized and bodies still in front of it, and I had to try to decide what to make for dinner.

Chapter Eight

I also bought my first car the summer we came home, a grey car I called simply The Chevy. Dad had bought it from a neighbour who had a bunch of kids and a sad wife and needed to leave town. He paid $35 for thirteen year old '62 Chevy station wagon, which had a newly re-built motor but not much else that worked.

I had been desperate for a car. The farm was twenty miles from town and I couldn't depend on the neighbours or Mom and Dad to haul me and four kids around. A car was freedom and independence. A car was one more step on the road to being my own person.

So now I had a car. Dad and my brother said reassuring things about the motor–slant six, they said, damn thing will never wear out. But I soon discovered the motor was about the only thing that worked. That and the headlights. The back seat was gone and the floor under the driver's seat had a hole in it that was great for disposing cherry pits and peanut shells. It was freezing in the winter; there was no heater and the back window wouldn't stay up. But with enough pillows and blankets and foamies and dogs, we survived.

One day I drove the Chevy up an almost vertical driveway to visit a woman my Dad had told me about. Some new people to the south of us, next to the old Mannarino place, were living in a tiny geodesic dome along with a couple of goats. They were living this marginal existence right next to two enormous geodesic domes they were building as a future home.

"You should get up there," my father growled at me one day. "That little woman needs some help. Damn shame to see a woman living like that. She's got a kid, too." I asked my kids about her son and they said, yes, he got on the school bus but they hadn't talked to him yet. He was a year older than them. His name was Adrian. He had long brown hair down to his shoulders and a serious thin face.

The woman, Carol, was living in a small, leaky dome beside two almost new, huge domes that her partner was building. But they couldn't move in, he had ordered, until the new domes were completely finished. No one in the Kootenays in those days finished their house. They got the frame up, or the dome or the logs or whatever it might be that they were building, and then they moved in. Everyone was living with pink insulation plastic-covered walls, no running water and wood stoves.

I stayed for tea and we wandered over to look at the new domes. "Why don't you move?" I said.

"Carl won't let us," she said. Carol always wore a scarf over her hair and she hid her beautiful blue eyes behind thick glasses. She looked down at the ground.

"Carl's having an affair," she whispered.

"Oh, I knew that, " I said. "Everyone knows. Everyone thinks he's a total jerk." Carol stared at me. I wished the words back. Now she would think I was the jerk, interfering in her life and spreading gossip.

But instead she smiled. " I didn't know what to say or who to ask for help."

"I'll help you move into your new place," I added. "Let's do it this weekend." And that weekend, to Carl's fury, Carol and her son moved into one of the new, unfinished geodesic domes that Carl had insisted had to be completely finished before they moved in.

After that, Carol's son Adrian started getting off the bus at my place and hanging out with the girls and Carol, Patti and I got into the habit of spending most of our time together. Somehow the kids were easier to manage in a pack and, if we pooled our money, our time and our resources, we felt less sorry for ourselves.

When winter came, the water in the trailer always froze. Carol didn't have running water either. Once a week, all winter long, we'd gather our kids along with a few other people's kids we'd somehow collected for the weekend; we would all bundle up and make the forty mile drive to Ainsworth Hot Springs. It meant we could all get

Chapter Eight

clean when our water was frozen.

The drive always turned into a three-hour marathon because we had to wait for the Kootenay Lake ferry. We loved the forty-five minute ferry ride from Kootenay Bay to the small community of Balfour, on the other side of the lake. After we drove on and parked, we all got out and went upstairs to the small coffee shop on the second floor. The kids ran wild, round and round, in and out the doors, while we drank coffee and gossiped with people we didn't see very often from that part of the lakeshore community. The ferry was always littered with lots of kids, running and screaming; we tried to pretend we didn't know them while the ferry guys rolled their eyes and disappeared into their own little room.

We always had just enough money to get to the Ainsworth Hot Springs, eleven miles north of the ferry landing, and pay our way in. We'd spend two or three hours in the pool. Mostly we sat in the steamy darkness of the cave at the back of the pool while the kids waded and swam. Often there was someone in the back of the cave playing a flute, or someone in a black grotto having sex, waves sloshing gently around them.

On the way home, everyone was always starving from the hours in the hot water. We usually had to pool our pennies to buy the kids some soup and French fries at the restaurant by the ferry. Once we thought we had the problem whipped because we brought along Patti's latest man, a rich boy from town with a white Corvette. God knows how she found him or what he thought of The Chevy. He didn't say. When we got to the restaurant, he watched us pooling pennies and counting change to buy each kid a bowl of mushroom soup, and then he ordered a double deluxe cheeseburger with fries for himself. None of us said a word. We watched him eat the whole thing. The kids watched each French fry disappear. It was too bad, I thought, that he never got to hear our sarcasm and hoots of laughter at his expense after he got in his Corvette to go home.

The kids and I would probably have gone hungry anywhere else, but we had the farm and my mother. In the summer, food literally dripped off the trees and bushes, raspberries squishing in the mud at the end of the rows where the irrigation ditches left puddles, the leftover cherries being hollowed out by wasps and ants, the plums and peaches and pears and apples and grapes we hadn't managed to sell or give away or turn into juice or freeze or can being squabbled over by ravens and robins and wasps. I grew an acre of vegetables every summer as well, and all summer long I carried boxes and buckets of produce to the farmer's market in town every week and stood in the blazing sun for half a day and came home twenty-five dollars or so richer.

The kids ran into my mother's kitchen after school for cookies, popcorn and hot chocolate. They stopped in there on their way to catch the school bus in the morning for treats for their lunches. Every Sunday Mom made dinner for the whole family; my brother came with his partner, and often my sister and her children, and we all carted home the leftovers.

I gradually got to know most of the new people. There was a sense of fellowship and community among these people who were, in a sense, a new wave of pioneers. Most of them had finally managed to buy land and were involved in building a house, raising children, growing gardens and coping with trying to figure out ways to make some money and still have time to create this new 'counterculture.'

For me, the counterculture was real and deeply felt; it reflected the values by which our family had always lived: being independent, self-sufficient and living a life centred around family, community, animals, gardening and nature. Now I didn't have to leave home to find my community. It was coming to me. For the first time in my life I had the sense of being part of a larger community. Although I had

Chapter Eight

quit using any kind of drugs long ago, I didn't mind that drugs and alcohol were part of it this new community. They were a bond of sorts, a means to an end, and a way of adding to the sense of freedom. Sharing a joint at a party was a ritual; dropping acid was a path to deeper understanding. I had done my share of it and I didn't regret it. It just wasn't interesting anymore. I had long ago learned any lessons that drugs had to teach.

After a while, on Sundays, people would start driving into my yard around noon, unloading food, dogs and kids. A soccer game or a baseball game would start up; the last dregs of the party would finish sometime around midnight.

When I was not working on the farm or visiting with people, I was reading. I had gone back to my habit of collecting books, despite my acute and usually desperate poverty. I'd first read about feminism when I was trapped in the southern US. I saw an ad for a women's collective who were helping abused women and I'd thought about phoning them but I hadn't.

Now feminism was in the news; one day I bought a book called *When God Was a Woman* by Merlin Stone. I read it all in one afternoon. I woke up from reading and thought, I've been lied to. It was like a cold clean wind blowing through my head, blowing out the humiliation and the embarrassment. For the first time I realized that what had happened to me, the abusive marriage, the children, the fear of university, hadn't all been my fault. My life was part of a larger pattern. It was an astonishing revelation. I hadn't just been ignorant and stupid. Although clearly I had made a lot of mistakes, perhaps if I began learning about what had happened to me, and why, I could prevent it ever happening again.

I began reading every feminist book I could find, which, in our little rural community, wasn't many. But there was a new bookstore in Nelson that I could get to occasionally and it had a shelf of books about women.

After I had read a few more of these books—Merlin Stone was followed by Robin Morgan, Ms. Magazine, Shulamith Firestone and Kate Millet's *Sexual Politics*, a book whose revelations and analysis ran like fire through my veins—I woke up to my need to talk to other women. It felt like my head was full of ideas, of conversations I had yet to have, of thoughts I needed to share.

Fortunately I had Carol; she and I talked incessantly. Our lives had run in similar paths: early pregnancy, early marriages that ended badly. Now we were single parent mothers and, more than anything else, we wanted a way out, some kind of path out of the welfare trap and into independence. Finally we decided to form a women's group. It was something I'd read about. After all, there were a lot of us, single moms on welfare, up and down the lake. The countercultural tide had washed into rural BC on a tide of idealism but, by 1977, it was already beginning to recede again, leaving a lot of wrecked relationships and women with small children behind.

We held our first women's meeting at Yvette's house. She was one of those people in the black truck who only spoke French. Once I had them sorted out, I found that Fred was Swiss and Yvette was French. They lived high up on the mountainside on the road that wound past the local dump. The house she and Fred had built together rested on posts set on a granite ridge, surrounded by huge cedar and fir. They couldn't yet afford insulation so, whenever I visited, we sat huddled around their wood cookstove with our feet in the oven.

Our first meeting was on a soft March day. The road up their hill had turned to deep yellow mush. One by one our cars slithered and roared and struggled up the driveway. Mud spurted onto my long skirt through the holes in the Chevy's floor. The kids hung on grimly as we lurched to a stop.

We parked among the boards and stumps in the steep driveway. Then Patti—of course, it was always Patti—managed to gun her way

Chapter Eight

almost up the whole hill before the Buick slithered to a halt, slid sideways and wedged itself against a cedar tree. We gathered around and stared at the car.

Someone named Yvonne said "We need help. I'll phone Barry."

"But this is a women's meeting," said Yvette. "Shouldn't we get it out ourselves?' We stared at the car some more. We weren't without resources. We got a jack and fitted it under the car, then jacked it up, heaved it sideways, did it again and then again. Just as we got the car back on the road, a man, a neighbour, arrived and took over although there was nothing left for him to do. We let him back the car down the hill and park it, while we went inside feeling satisfied with ourselves and drank tea and sat around the stove for the rest of the afternoon until it was time to sort out our own kids from the screaming herd and take them home for supper.

That night as I made supper in the trailer, with music on the stereo, the woodstove clucking and snapping, the kids gathered around the table, the light over their heads keeping off the darkness from the outside, I began to feel—for the first time in a very long time—safe in my life. I had friends and I some sense of purpose. I was still terrified that the boys' father would come after them again; I was conscious that I was probably guilty of kidnapping, a felony in the US, if he bothered to pursue me. I had made up my mind that whatever I had to do, he would never find me and my children; we would hide, we would run, I would do whatever I had to do to keep them safe. I was often an inattentive mother; for example, I woke from reading Lord of the Rings one day to find the kids had piled all the chairs in the trailer around me and I hadn't noticed. But I was always a grizzly-bear mother as well, ready to defend my children from any threat, real or perceived.

That was our first women's meeting but we held many more over the next couple of years. People in the community thought it was a great joke and the men, including my father, made endless nasty references to hen parties and women sitting around gossiping when there was work to be done, but we didn't care any more. Something had changed. We knew we made them nervous and we didn't mind a bit. We were serious, or some of us were, even though every week we had another argument about what it was we were actually doing or why or how. But it was important. I was beginning to realize I had a lot to figure out. I began to realize there was a lot that no one had told me.

Carol, Patti and I also did a lot of talking on our own. Patti used to tell us stories of her epic fights with her husband; once he shot up her car with a rifle and that was the last straw: she packed up her daughter, took his truck and left. After that she kept moving to stay away from him. She told us she had once moved sixteen times in one year.

One night she relented after he phoned and begged to be allowed to see their daughter. This time he got drunk and took an axe to her car. But it so happened that the night he did this, all our kids were watching out the windows with mystified fascination. Carol and I talked her into calling the police, but they seemed more interested in the damage to the car than any threat to her.

I was hoping the boys' father, whom I had left behind and far away, would drink himself to death and leave us alone permanently. Carol said she was determined to stop falling in love with men who looked interesting but were actually crazy; her last partner had moved his new girlfriend, then his girlfriend's brother, then his girlfriend's mother, into the other half of the geodesic dome he shared with Carol. He said he was founding a new way of life. Carol just thought the whole thing was embarrassing.

Despite our developing sense of feminism, we also lived in hope that we'd all get smart enough and meet men wonderful enough that we'd be tempted to try having a relationship one more time. But we'd be careful, we told each other. Very careful. We dreamed of nice men,

Chapter Eight

fatherly men, men who would like our kids and want to hang around with them and with us and provide them with toys and double cheeseburgers with fries and all the other things we couldn't afford. We talked a lot about how we might meet these new kinds of men because there weren't any around that we knew.

Good fathers were important, we believed. Our kids needed a good father image, good role models, unlike their real fathers. And of course, men were good for other things—they fixed cars and stereos and washing machines. They could build houses. And there was sex, which we hardly ever talked about. But we all thought about it.

The other, partnered-up, men in the community were nice to us. Sometimes they helped out but they had enough to cope with. We made them uneasy. I think they thought I was doing fine; I was mostly an amusing spectacle with my Chevy full of kids and dogs and laundry and vegetables. Eventually I parked the Chevy and, with the money I had scrounged from selling vegetables, I bought a Ford truck. The motor burned oil so my Dad found someone to help me rebuild the motor. Every day for weeks I fiddled around with things called valves and rings. I never had a clue what I was doing. What terrified me was how many parts a motor had and how fragile the whole thing seemed to be. But then I put it all back together again and amazingly, it ran and ran well with a few minor hitches.

Once I arrived at my friend Joan's house with a boiling-over radiator on my wonderful truck. She was married to my childhood buddy, Alan Wilson—our youngest sons were the same age—and they made the best coffee in the country. They were in the process of building their house.

I went inside for help. Alan and three or four other men were drinking coffee and discussing the niceties and particularities of septic tank fields, a topic that all the men in the community seemed to find endlessly engrossing. It was either that or the iniquities of different kinds of chainsaws that formed the bulk of their conversations.

When I explained about the truck, they strode outside and stood around in the hot sun discussing what to do. Joan and I drank coffee and gossiped. When they had things all figured out and fixed, they all tromped back in. I had to listen to a lecture on checking the water level in the radiator and leaky hoses that should be replaced and not merely taped up with duct tape but what the hell. The radiator always leaked. I'd just been too busy that day to put water in it.

Carol and I talked endlessly about what to do with our lives. She wanted a label, she said, any label that would stick, that would give her assurance, social respectability and a job.

Maybe we could go back to school, we thought, but what could we study that would guarantee us a real job and a good living and how could we ever manage school with our kids and all the schools being far away at the coast?

And, of course, I still desperately wanted to be a writer, which seemed as unlikely as becoming an astronaut. The social worker who drove out from town once a year just sighed when she saw the trailer and the kids and the chaos we lived in. She also turned a blind eye to the few hundred dollars I made in the summer from the garden. But what would happen when the kids were all in school? I'd have to get a job then, she said reprovingly. The government wouldn't pay for me to just sit around and raise my kids. But neither would they pay for university. They might, she said, pay for a one-year course somewhere as long as it guaranteed me employment at the end. I didn't want to sit around on welfare either. I wanted them to pay my way through university. I went for employment testing at the local government agency. The bored man behind the desk asked me what I did. I described my life, gardening and picking fruit.

"Perhaps you could get a job mowing lawns or looking after gardens," he said. But I wanted to give my kids someone, something, to live up to. A life of mowing lawns wasn't in my plans.

I kept working as hard as I could. Every spring I ordered a box

Chapter Eight

of seeds and started baby plants under grow lights in my parent's basement. By the end of February I'd start pruning the apple and peach trees and by March it would be time to start the tomato and pepper seedlings for the garden. About the beginning of April, my father would plow a large plot of land, beside the highway, that had once been our raspberry patch. Around the middle of April, I started planting a market garden about a hectare in size. I usually finished planting by the end of May. Everything got planted in succession so that as one patch of lettuce or peas or spinach finished, another would be ripening. I experimented with all kinds of crops: soybeans, peanuts and Jerusalem artichokes, among others.

There were always the usual summer chores of picking fruit and getting in the hay. I bought a food drier and a freezer, plus my mother and I canned fruit together. In my spare moments I swam and lay on the beach reading books on women's issues, or hung out with Carol and Joan and Patti, talking, talking, talking.

Winters were difficult and never got any easier. I chopped wood and tried to keep the trailer warm and clean and the kids clean and fed and get them, every morning, onto the yellow school bus by 8 am. I began to go to meetings, peace meetings and environmental meetings. Nat, my youngest son, still headed off for his grandmother's every morning after the other kids caught the bus, so I had an hour alone.

I tried to start writing a novel. I realized that I had no idea how to write despite the fact that I had been writing poems and journals in secret for years.

I knew the time was coming when I would have to make some decisions about the rest of my life but I kept shoving it away. One warm spring morning in early May, I put on Dvorak's *New World* symphony and opened the doors and windows. I shook out the rugs and took the ashes out of the stove and set the houseplants outside and rinsed the dust off them. I vacuumed the whole house and, as I danced with the vacuum and sang with the music, I began to be happy. Daffodils and tulips were blooming at the front of the trailer; the alder and birch were haloed in electric green mist.

It was a fine morning to be alive and to be dancing and singing in the misty green sunshine. It was enough to be alive as the trees and flowers were alive, demanding nothing, simply alive and radiating joy in it. I danced outside and sang along to the trees. The universe unfolded around me radiant, a huge white flower, unfolding into a stupendous infinity in which I still danced. After a while I came back to myself sitting on a rock in the sun, with ants crawling up my ankles. I went back in and finished the vacuuming.

The next morning, when I picked up the mail from the green box across the road, there were three things in it: a Sears catalogue, a gardening catalogue, and a university calendar sent by a friend. I looked through them all. The Sears one was full of stuff I couldn't afford and didn't really want; the gardening catalogue was full of seeds and ideas for bigger and better gardens. Just looking at it made me tired. The university calendar was from the University of Victoria, on Vancouver Island, 800 kilometres away. They offered a degree in Creative Writing. I didn't know it was possible to study Creative Writing in university. I had been considering going to college to take a course in forestry or welding, anything with which to get a job. But now all those fine practical ideas went out the window. I was going to go. I had no money, I had four children, I would never make any money as a writer, I didn't even know if I could write. I was going to go.

Chapter Nine

I MET SOMEONE, a man my children took to immediately, who fixed my truck, along with things in the trailer that made him shake his head in horror, like the bare wires of the cord from the TV stuck into a socket. And he wasn't a stranger; he was one of the beach kids that I had known vaguely when I was a kid but never paid any attention to, someone who loved boats and the lake. Mostly I had played with his sisters but I hadn't known Len well because he was shy and spent much of his time working on his rowboat. Now he was building a house down the road from the farm, something I also knew but, because he hadn't come to any of the parties at my house, our paths hadn't crossed recently.

We met at Joan and Alan's house; we talked and went for walks and a friendship grew between us that began to turn into a relationship. He was warm and kind and supportive and finally I told him about going back to university.

"That's a crazy idea," he said. "Why would you want to do that?"

"I have to go. I have to get off welfare. I have to at least try to be a writer. Otherwise I'll never know if I can do it."

We spent the evening and the next few weeks discussing and arguing about it. Finally he agreed, very reluctantly, to come with me. By now he was spending his nights at the trailer and the kids had decided they had a real parent. He bought them goofy presents they loved, took them to movies and fixed their bikes. In no time they were spending every spare moment with him. But he had been dreaming of finishing his house and living on his own land. He had been living with his sister and brother-in-law, working part-time and trying to manage, in his spare time, to put up another round of logs on his house. Money was always a problem for both of us.

Every month I picked up a cheque for $450 from the welfare office in Creston and put $200 of it in the bank. Previously, whenever it was cheque day, I bought two sets of treats, art supplies for the kids and a book and some magazines for me. And I bought food treats that we only had once a month, like oranges and ice cream and chocolate.

Now I only bought the barest necessities and not much of that. Most of our food came from the farm anyway, and now Len made up for the rest, taking the kids to movies and out to dinner. I was astounded and endlessly grateful for the generosity of this warm kind man. I was also amazed and grateful that he was going to move with us. I knew that going to school as a single parent with four children would be next to impossible. Being with Len made the dream more of a reality.

Finally, one day in late August, we packed up my truck and his car and left the farm for Victoria. The kids stared out the window for a last glimpse of the farm and their grandma. The two cats and the dog huddled together in the back seat. We settled into a basement apartment in Victoria; I found a part-time daycare for Nat, who was

Chapter Nine

just starting kindergarten and, finally, I set off for my first creative writing classes at the University of Victoria. I had never been more terrified.

I took my poetry, that I had been writing in secret for years, and submitted one of my poems to the first poetry class I took. We had been asked to submit them anonymously. The next class, I drove my truck through two red lights on my way to University. The cop who stopped me was laughing. He walked around the truck. "You've got bald tires and no brake lights," he said.

"I'm going to school," I said. "I can't be late. It's my first class. We are talking about my poem this morning."

He shook his head. "Well, I'll let you off with a warning this time."

When I got to school I got a cup of coffee and a donut. I had been writing for years in fifteen-minute segments in the local bakery while my laundry went round and round in the dryers next door and I was addicted to the smell of sugar and coffee. When I got to class the professor shuffled papers around until we got started. Finally he held up a poem that I recognized as my own.

He sighed deeply. "This is just a really bad T.S. Eliot imitation," he said. My breath stuck in my chest. The other people chimed in with their criticisms but I couldn't hear anything. There was a roaring in my ears, a red mist in front of my eyes. What did he mean? Eventually the red mist began to clear and I began to listen. He was going over my terrible poem line by line, pointing out its strengths, pointing out its weaknesses. I looked at my own copy. He was right. There was a way of thinking here, a language that I didn't understand but I could learn. Everything in a poem needs a reason to be there, he said and you need to understand what that reason is. I would learn this, I thought. Somehow I would figure it out.

When I went home, I picked up my youngest son from his new daycare. I carried him down the block to our new basement apartment. The sun was shining and anything was possible. And finally I was going to learn how to be a writer.

My two years at UVic were extraordinarily happy. The kids ended up loving Victoria, after they discovered the swimming pool, the library and the mall. And I loved UVic despite their (then) philosophy that if you were tough enough to survive their program, you were tough enough to become a Canadian writer. They also told their mostly female students not to write that 'women's stuff,' that touchy-feely stuff, that "confessional" writing, as it was then termed. It was 1979. UVic had just started a Women's Studies program. I took Women's Studies and Creative Writing and ran happily through the halls of UVic on my way to my wonderful classes.

After two years I had a degree in Creative Writing and a sheaf of poems and stories. Len and I loaded up our new-ancient white van and drove back up the mountain passes to the Kootenays. We had spent two years in the city dreaming of going home. We were still committed to the idea of land, of homesteading, independence and self-sufficiency. My friend and classmate, Julian Ross, who wanted to start a publishing company, offered to publish my first book of poems. His company, he said, would be called Polestar Books.

We arrived at the house-site on a late evening with everything we owned packed into the van. The house, which Len had been working on for a couple of years before we moved away, had a floor, four walls, and a roof. That was it. We unpacked what we could in the dark and put up our new tent, bought cheaply the day before in Vancouver. We unrolled sleeping bags and blankets, let the cats and the dog out of the van, and went to bed. In the sunny morning the kids flitted like bright birds around the flat clearing below the house, while I made breakfast over the fire and tried to figure out where we were going to put everything. There was a small travel trailer parked in the clearing; Len had used it to store his tools. It was musty and full of spiders and mildew but would do for storage—for now. The boys would sleep with us in the tent. The girls could sleep in the van.

The sun shone hot while I set up a camp of sorts, banged nails into the trees, stacked some bricks and boards for shelves. Alan and Joan came and we sat on logs around the fire, drinking smoky tea. Yes, we said, we were glad to be home, out of the city, back in the woods, back in our home community. The kids weren't so sure. They'd gotten used to the swimming pool, the library and the movies. They loved going to the mall, or London Drugs for snacks after a movie. They loved our carpeted apartment, the corner store, the streets down which they could ride bikes and skateboards. Only Len and I had hated it. Or so we thought.

I knelt on the ground with my face in the smoke and cooked and, in the morning, I shook out our sleeping bags and tried to be glad I was home, to love our new place, which was only five miles from the farm and my parents. Len's sister and brother-in-law were our nearest neighbours, we knew everyone, we knew every inch of the place. I was home, I told myself, so why was I so restless?

Every day I went for a walk with the dogs and looked around. However familiar it was, it was still a new place, a new mountainside and new trails on which to walk. And slowly the reality of what we were doing began to sink in. We had no jobs and only a bit of money that disappeared like magic in one visit to the building supply store. Len could always make money surveying, but jobs for women in the nearby small town of Creston were specific. Women were still, in that logging and farming-based town, even in the early eighties, confined to being secretaries or cooks or nurses or teachers. We were almost immediately trapped into the eternal dilemma of homesteading or of people who wanted to be homesteaders, now or in the past. Homesteading, house building, acquiring tools and animals, even planting a garden—all of them take immense amounts of time and some amount of money. However cheaply we tried to do it, the house was going to cost money as well. And however basically we tried to live, we had four growing, eating, demanding children who wanted more than anything else to live in a real house with normal parents.

So we camped outside and the kids got up in the morning, got dressed out of packs and struggled down the hill to catch the school bus. It was April but relatively warm and we could take showers and baths at my parents' house.

Then two things happened: one day, in early May, we watched a towering white wall of dust moving north up the valley. Mount St. Helens had blown up the day before and the dust had taken a day to reach us. The dust left a sticky, inch-thick layer of grit over everything and then it began to rain.

We moved into the house that evening. Len ran a line from the power pole and hooked up an electric heater. I hung a blanket over the table and we sat around it shivering in our coats with blankets and sleeping bags over our shoulders. That night we slept on the gritty, sawdust-laden plywood floor and began our new life in our house.

Our land was mountainside, unsuitable for farming or gardening or anything other than growing trees or brush, but with four young children, we needed a yard and a garden. My father came with his backhoe and Len had an ancient Cat and, for a week, they felled trees, pulled stumps and went back and forth on their machines, tearing up the ground.

I was thrilled and excited about this—we needed a garden and, even though I recognized that we had moved into someone else's habitat, I figured our small piece of land wasn't too intrusive. After all, the bears, coyotes, deer and elk had the rest of the mountainside above us, what wasn't logged or burnt over. I worked beside the machines all one day, piling branches against the stumps so we could have a good big fire when everything dried out, picking rocks and sticks and clods of brush out of the gray mountain soil.

Chapter Nine

But the noise of the machines bothered me. The Cat made a high-pitched squeal that sound like a child crying far away. It kept surprising me. I'd be working away and then I'd hear this baby crying and I'd look up but it was just the machines, snorting and puffing away and belching blue smoke into the air. After a while I went in the house but I could still hear it, over and above the machine noise, even through the thick log walls of our house. I was relieved when the machines quit and I could get down to what I knew best: planting, weeding, mulching and harvesting.

After we first moved in, bears and coyotes used to come by to see what we were doing to the neighbourhood, but they soon found out we weren't such good neighbours—too many dogs and too much noise and smoke—and stayed away.

But the ospreys, beautiful brown and white fishhawks, came; there were at least four osprey nests close to the house because below the mountainside on which our place was perched were about 3000 acres of wetlands—a diked-off wildlife reserve at the south end of Kootenay Lake. Whenever we went for a walk on the mountain or to the neighbouring farm the ospreys followed us, winging in lazy circles over our heads unless one of us pointed a camera or binoculars at them and then they'd somehow disappear straight up into thin air until they were only tiny black specks in the high atmosphere. As soon as the camera or binoculars disappeared, they'd return, playing and sliding back and forth on invisible wind currents. They didn't mind us. All they needed was fish and wind and a tall tree in which to put a nest. I often thought, however anthropomorphically, that they must feel sorry for us, so earthbound and slow.

We had every right, we thought as well, to tear up the ground and the trees and make a garden. We played at being pioneers, doing everything by hand, living with an outhouse, no running water, scrounging food from my parent's farm and growing bits of our own.

Farming was what I knew and what I wanted; although I realized early on that this mountain clearing would never be a farm, it could be a home.

Eventually we made a place for ourselves that the kids and Len and I all loved—a kind of fortress refuge place, a log house perched on the edge of a cliff, with a lawn and fruit trees and garden in a hollow behind it, and then the mountain rising sharply, just past the edge of the lawn, where skinny fir trees leaned over our driveway. Our neighbours were far enough away that we couldn't hear them. Even the noise from the highway below was distant and muffled. The main noises were birds, ducks, swans and geese in the swamp and, at night, the wind in the tall firs. Our driveway was actually the remains of the old 'tote' road, which still ran along the mountainside for about five miles.

The dilapidated but still intact log cabin on our nearest neighbour's piece of land had belonged to Alan's grandfather. The land we lived on was originally part of his land grant, about 800 acres of mountainside and swamp. The highway below us had once been a railway bed. Vestiges of recent history were all around us. The trees on our land had grown up past the tall, still-standing stumps left by the first loggers.

But there were few signs of the life that aboriginal people had once lived in this area. Along the shores of Kootenay Lake, on flat granite rock faces, are drawings made with red ochre. There was one by the beach where I had grown up. It was on Redman's Point– a pictograph of a red man with a halo around his head that looked like sunrays. Just past the point, under a shelf of overhanging rocks, was another set of faded pictographs.

Little is known about the pictographs, which are hidden on rock faces and boulders up and down both sides of the lakes throughout the Kootenays. I once asked a Ktunaxa elder about them and he laughed gently and said maybe they were places people went to have

Chapter Nine

visions or dreams or maybe they were just good places to hang out and catch fish.

One of the legends about Kootenay Lake is that the native people never lived there—they went there to fish, to hunt, to catch sturgeon, but they didn't live there because the energy was too strong. The same legend floats around about other places—about Nelson, or New Denver—to explain why the Sinixt people who once lived there left and went south. But new research and writers, such as Eileen Delehanty Pearkes in Nelson, have demonstrated that this legend is European wishful thinking. The Sinixt were pushed off their land by settlers, miners and disease. The Ktunaxa were confined to a small reserve near Creston and their numbers were also decimated, both by disease and by the wholesale forcible adoption of many of their children during the fifties and sixties.

My first poetry book came out. Julian Ross made good on his promise. He organized a book launch and a party in Victoria and my friend Joan came with me. We drove the long drive, back down out of the mountains to the lower mainland of BC and across the Strait of Georgia on the giant BC ferry, to Victoria. People congratulated both me and Julian. For the first time in my life I felt the possibility of writing as an actual career, not just a dream. But I was also terrified of the book, of the label 'writer', of the judgment of real writers who I was sure were somewhere out there in the world, laughing at my efforts. And then we got back in our tiny red Ford Cortina that coughed as it trundled its way back up the five mountain passes between the coast and the Kootenays. We came over the Blueberry-Paulsen pass in a blinding snowstorm late at night but, finally, we made it home. I went back to being a mother, a housewife, a gardener and a farmer.

As always, the mountains called me out every day to walk. I had always been a walker, ever since I started running away in Riondel when I was three. There is a powerful pleasure in walking through country that is always familiar and always new. All my life, when I came home from school—after tea with my mother—I would go first to the lake. There was always a moment, every day, when I came out of the trees and onto the lakeshore, the sun bouncing off the water and rocks, hitting my eyes, waking me up when I knew it was beautiful. Every day I knew it again. If I couldn't walk, if I couldn't see the land, I felt as if I couldn't breathe.

Near our place there was a little bump on the side of the mountain above the highway, called Mt. Pedro. From there I could look north, could see my parent's farm squatted five miles away below the spine of the mountain that ended in Red Man's Point. I could see west over the river channel below, into the swamp past the fringe of brittle cottonwoods where there was a golden eagle's nest I could never find, though I was pretty sure I knew where it ought to be.

A lot of animals came up to the bald and mossy top of Mt. Pedro. Perhaps they liked the view. There was nothing else to tempt them up there. In winter there was always a line of deer tracks and coyote tracks coming up through the long slope of moss on the north side. Mt. Pedro wasn't actually on our land and, at one point, it was bought by someone who announced to the community that he was going to use it for 'vision quests'. When I went up there, after we moved back from University, there was a round circle of rocks in the middle of the one grassy flat place.

Now, when we were younger, my brother and I had gone to great effort to make sure that every loose rock we could find had been rolled off the top of Mt. Pedro. In fact, at one point, we'd even brought crowbars with us to make doubly sure. One side of the mountain was sheer cliff, with a gully at the bottom that caught the rocks before they hit the road. Our ambition was to somehow roll a rock big enough so it would go through the gully and hit the road, but we never did.

Chapter Nine

It took me most of the afternoon to roll those rocks off the cliff and into the gully and some of them were huge. I was amazed that someone had managed to get them up the hill and onto the top of Mt. Pedro. But I doubted he would try it again.

I went there almost every day. After we had stared around for a while, the dogs and I would pick our way down the northern side of Mt.Pedro, through the thick grey-green moss that layered its slick granite, down through the cedars, across the highway and into the swamp at the south end of the lake.

The swamp was a place of never-ending exploration for the dogs and me; the clay bank by the river was full of holes where the beavers denned, the willow thickets sheltered herds of whitetail deer. We would wander past the Rat Slough, full of rattling cattails, across Boulder Creek, through the slim new forest of alder and cottonwood that had grown up since the lake levels were changed by the building of the Libby Dam, then out onto the long finger of sand and mud that stretched out from the mouth of the river into the lake itself. There was always a wind blowing and the lake stretched away like an ocean.

Once, when I was small and we were all out looking for the cows, my father brought us to this riverbank in the boat. He landed us on this sandy bank and handed us poles.

"Don't stand in one place," he said, "or you'll sink."

It was true; if I stood in one place long enough, water would seep through the thin skin of dried mud and I would begin to sink. I could make vast sinkholes of mud in the sandbar just by moving my feet every few minutes. When I jumped up and down, the whole sandbar shook like jelly.

I would always make it home from these expeditions by the time the kids got off the school bus and then, after they had exploded into the house in a welter of lunch kits and jackets, after the TV and the stereo had both gone on and they eaten whatever snacks and food I had set out for them, I would go outside to work in the garden until it was time to make dinner.

For, as much as I loved the house, the land, the garden, our fortress oasis, I was restless and I couldn't make the restlessness go away. Words and stories and poems came and, just as quickly, went. Sometimes I wrote in the mornings after the kids left, but the house was such chaos, spilled milk and cereal dripping off the counters, at least two loads of laundry to be done every day and hung out to dry, dishes piled in stacks on the still unfinished counters, beds to be made, flies and dust and sawdust and piles of paper to be gotten rid of, the woodstove to be filled, wood to be split and carried in, that I could only steal an hour or so before my conscience got the better of me. And outside there were the chickens, the garden, the lawn and the flowerbeds. My mother phoned every day to see if I wanted to come for coffee. She was lonely but my mother had always been lonely.

Sometimes I wrote at night or I wrote in the bathtub. I put things in the mail, poems, and stories that sometimes got published. Whenever I went to town for groceries I always went to the bakery. There was something about the irresistible combination of coffee and sugar and the hum of conversation that would let me write. But I could only steal half an hour away; there was always much to be done, usually some kids needing to be picked up from soccer lessons or golf lessons or music lessons.

There is also something deadly and disheartening about sitting in a bakery in the middle of a grey afternoon, with country music coming through the scratchy speakers, with trucks grumbling by on the pavement still dusty with leftover grit and salt from winter, with the usual tables full of retired elderly men who met there every afternoon or mothers with small fussing children stuffing their mouths with sugar or, occasionally, people like me, sitting alone and staring out the window. But I was always the only one with a notebook or even a book.

Chapter Nine

I watched the trucks and the tourists race by on their way to somewhere else. There was always somewhere else. There was still so much I didn't know. I didn't know about the world or about how to be a writer or about how to be a part of something.

On every trip to town I went to the library. I kept a list of books on order at the library. The librarian usually disappeared into her office when I showed up, leaving a volunteer to deal with my endless requests. Fortunately, one of the library volunteers was my former high school English teacher who sympathized with my need for books. The nearest bookstore was two hours away and, whenever I got a chance, I went there and bought books and magazines I couldn't afford. Books piled up beside the bed, spilled over onto the floor, climbed up the walls, threatened to become compost on the floor. I read and read into the night while Len, exhausted from working all day and building the house in his spare time, slept beside me.

I read in the morning while I got the kids off to school and I read in the bathtub or in the car when I was waiting for someone to get out of soccer practice and I read while I was waiting anywhere for anything.

There were no jobs in the town. Occasionally I got a few part-time jobs but they never lasted. A job came up at one of the local papers and I sent in my resume. The editor called me to come and see her.

I went in her office and sat down.

"You know we can't hire you," she said. "I think you understand why."

No, I didn't, actually. I was the only person I knew in the area with an actual degree in writing and journalism. Was that what she meant? I stared at her. She wouldn't meet my eyes. I left, knowing there was nothing to be said. Whoever she thought I was, or whatever box in her head I didn't fit into, couldn't be changed.

The other newspaper in town was dying. I worked there for a

while. I threw out all the whiskey bottles stashed in various drawers and stayed up all night writing the entire paper on the ancient phototypesetter that spit out long strips of paper that were then waxed and laid on the layout sheets. Eventually I added up the revenue from the few ads that were still coming in and the cost of actually printing the paper. They were far apart in the wrong direction.

A new woman had come to town. She was working for the other newspaper. She called me one day to ask if I wanted to help her organize a women's conference. "We'll make it about women and writers, like that women and words conference they had at the coast" she said.

"How do we do that?"

"The government will give us money," she said. I was amazed. I couldn't imagine the government doing such a thing.

The new woman didn't stay long. She was far too smart and far too ambitious. She went off and got a job at the *Vancouver Sun*. She left me with an unfinished grant application and a desperate desire to be part of a women writers' community. I drove to Cranbrook to the women's centre to see if any of this fantastic idea was even possible. I spent the afternoon there and came home with an application asking the government to send me $10,000 to organize a conference on women and words, part of which would pay me to do such a thing. Apparently I had to have something called a board so I asked various friends if they would call themselves board members. Since I assured them it wouldn't be any work, they all agreed.

I had no idea how to organize a conference but I figured it out one step at a time. In the spring of 1984 I booked all the rooms in a motel in downtown Creston, organized speakers, made a budget, hired caterers, advertised the thing and waited with some terror to see if anyone would show up. Women did—they came from all over the Kootenays. They came to the workshops, applauded the speakers, thronged to the dinner, ate the lunch and went home again. I spent the whole weekend in a daze, appalled and delighted at what I had done.

When the conference was done I fled with relief back to the mountainside, to our unfinished log house, and back to walking, brooding, reading and trying to bring order into the chaos of six people living in a small unfinished log house with no running water.

But the idea had caught on. A group of women wanted to do the whole thing all over again in Nelson. I began going there two or three times a week, a long two-hour drive each way. Usually I caught the last ferry home and usually I was the only car on the last ferry, driving the thirty miles home through untracked snow, crawling along, following my own lights through the blackness up the hill to the warmth and silence of home.

I had a computer by now. And we finally had running water. The fall before we had hand dug our way through a quarter mile of rotten granite and dirt, laid the black plastic pipe in the trench, covered it with sawdust and filled it in. It was a miracle: no more heating water on the stove in the mornings so the kids could wash their hair, no more hauling water in plastic buckets, no more trips to the outhouse in the middle of the freezing night.

The second conference went well. I read some poetry. After I finished reading, the audience all stood up and applauded. I fled the stage, the applause, the attention. I ended the evening wandering through the empty rooms of the college where we had organized the conference, struggling in a drunken daze to remember how to lock everything up, going to my room and doubling over with anguish and nausea and fear. Who had those people been applauding? One of the women at the conference was a well-known writer–she had congratulated me on my poetry, she had held my hand and looked into my eyes and said, "Send me some work. I'd like to read it."

When I went home this time I tried to go back to walking and doing laundry and making dinner but a new person was looking out of my eyes. A new person lay in bed every night, reading, turning over, restless, sometimes getting up to go downstairs and read by the fire, thinking about the poet who had held my hand, thinking about poetry.

Even when I went walking, shadows followed me. I tried to outwalk them but they ran ahead of me. Some days the discontent lifted and I could breathe.

I went back to what I had done in high school, wandering through the woods looking for silence, trying to connect to the other inhabitants of the mountain we lived on. I had been practicing walking up to animals for most of my life, cows and horses and then wild animals, porcupines, skunks and wasps.

I had first discovered this ability from the hours spent in the orchard picking fruit. When the cherries or plums got over-ripe, every insect in the neighbourhood smelled the call to food and when my father insisted we pick the stuff, we shared the tree with wasps, hornets, fat bumblebees, ants and many other types of flying crawling creatures. Under these conditions, each piece of fruit became a negotiation; if I went slowly, asked by moving my hand for permission, the wasps and hornets would amiably move over and give me room. It was a tense process; I hated getting stung. I swelled up for weeks, my stung arm or hand turned bright red and fiery with itch. But after a while, I got blasé about hornets and wasps. I used to sit still and let them crawl on my arms and hands, or put my head down on the table and watch them eat pieces of fruit, chewing methodically from side to side with their strong tiny jaws.

When my husband and I began building our log house it was a dry hot summer. There were yellow jacket nests everywhere; the kids got caught once crawling through the brush below the house and my youngest son came home with dozens of stings.

When I went for a walk I listened carefully for the angry buzz that would let me know there was a nest. There was pile of lumber near the house that needed to be moved and, as soon as I went close to it, I saw one or two black hornets flying lazy circles in the summer sun. Soon I located the nest, hanging underneath the edge of a board, a paper castle, a domed retreat of shadow and myriad hidden passages. As I went closer a few more hornets came out and flew in circles around me, a couple landed on my clothes and crawled up hands and arms, smelling and testing this intruder. When I stepped back, they left. Their language was a precise etymology of space and distance. I began visiting the nest on a regular basis that summer and, on each visit, they allowed me to get a bit closer. I would sit on the ground, a couple of feet from the nest, as they went about their private hornet lives. When fall came I didn't go back for a while and, when I did, the nest was a dry, rattling, empty husk.

I began to realize that, in building our house and clearing trees, we had profoundly affected the neighbourhood. Every fall the orchard next door on the Mannarino place attracted bears–they had been coming there since my parents abandoned the place; now my children got off the school bus every day and walked up the long hill past the orchard. One day they began telling me about the twin bear cubs that met them every day after school. They said the cubs seemed to want to play.

The next day I called the dogs and wandered down the long hill, under the yellowing alders and maples, past the orchard. The dogs took off barking and the mother bear streaked across the road in front of me. She paced beside me, just inside the trees, chopping her jaws, so I called the dogs back, grabbed them by their collars, and went on down the hill, assuming she would leave.

But when the kids piled down off the bus and we started up the hill she was still there, pacing back and forth across the road. Since a gaggle of kids, two dogs and a grown human are a lot for an angry black bear to withstand, I knew something else was up. I sent the kids and the dogs back down the hill and looked around until I spotted the two small bundles of black fur high up in an enormous fir tree that leaned out over the road.

"Get your babies," I called to her, with no faith that she understood the words. Knowing she would understand a language of distance, I retreated slowly down the hill, still talking and, when I was far enough away, she went to the fir tree and bawled to the babies, who skidded down the tree as fast as they could go. Then her family disappeared into the trees and my family and I went home as well. We never saw her again.

Animals floated in and through our lives all the time. A myriad of stray dogs, cats, horses and even chickens, came and stayed.

The chickens, in particular, created their own strange ecosystem. Someone gave us a few Bantam chickens and we stuck them into their newly prepared chicken house, from which they promptly escaped. One by one, that spring, they disappeared and I assumed that a skunk, a weasel or a coyote had done away with them and then, one by one, they reappeared, followed by a dozen or so adorably fluffy and cute baby chicks. A bantie mother is a formidably dedicated creature with a lot of enemies. The hawks and owls and eagles from the swamp circled our small yard; ravens sat in the fir trees above the driveway and yelled messages to each other about the free food. While the chicks were small, the mothers kept them under brush and under cover. The dogs and I kept watch during the day and at night I herded those chicks and mothers I could find into the chicken shed and locked them up. But as the chicks grew, the mothers became more determined to teach them how to roost properly, as bantie chickens should, in a tree.

Nightly the owls came and nightly chickens disappeared but bantie mothers are both persistent and prolific. And I was

Chapter Nine

determined. I strung twine and nets over the bushes; grimly every night I tried to herd them back into their safe warm chicken shed. Despite the nightly owl raids, new bantie mothers kept appearing from under boards and bushes with new hoards of baby chicks. I came out of the house one afternoon and looked into the trees. Our silent yard was ringed by hawks, sitting in the tops of trees. The chickens were all squatting under cover. As I stood in the middle of the yard a small hawk, obviously overwrought by the situation, launched itself at my head. It pulled up at the last minute when it realized I wasn't a chicken but its wings grazed my cheek. It sounded like a small jet as it went by.

I borrowed a 22 rifle from my father but I felt ridiculous, sitting out there guarding my chickens. In fact I couldn't really decide whose side I was on, the hawks or the chickens. I had created an ecological nightmare and it was just going to have to play itself out. Which it did, slowly. After a while the chicken population dwindled to a few discouraged individuals that I managed to keep penned in the shed. The hawks and owls went away. I took the rifle back. I realized I didn't have the heart to make a real farm here in the woods. I was squatting in someone else's home.

I had started a novel and it crawled on. Outside the world was full of ferment. I read more magazines, more books. I was still going to meetings, peace meetings and environmental meetings. Every day I looked at the beauty of the world I walked through–then I read images of terror and pain. Nuclear weapons, ecological devastation, women marching on Ottawa, meetings and letters and dead animals and visions of mushroom clouds. One night I found my son hiding under his bed.

"Why are you sleeping under there?"

"In case of the bomb," he said.

I promised him—it was all I could do—that I wouldn't let the bombs fall.

From our house perched on the cliff I looked out over the second-growth fir trees at the river, at the cottonwoods and reedbeds beyond it, at the railway that crossed the Kootenay River, to the distant reach of Kootenay Lake and the blue heights of the Selkirk Mountains. I would imagine a world where people were busy changing things. I wanted to be part of that. There had been a group in the town that I used to go to when the kids and I were on our own, the Survival Group it was called. In it were several teachers, who used to be my high school teachers and other people I had gone to school with, as well as my friend Carol. It was my first experience of belonging to a political organization and it was the first time I found out that if you volunteered for something, you could end up, pretty fast, being in charge of it.

At that time, BC Hydro had a plan to build a diversionary canal between the Kootenay River and the Columbia River where they flow down out of the Rocky Mountains within a mile of each other. On paper in Vancouver, the plan probably made sense. It would have sent a lot more water flowing through the dams on the Columbia River, both in Canada and the US, and that would, of course, generate more power. It made financial sense as well, as long as no one took into account the flooding of a hundred miles of productive wetland that fills the valley bottom from Canal Flats to Golden. Or what would happen to Kootenay Lake if it suddenly lost eighty percent of its water flow. We began to write letters and hold meetings, driving hundreds of miles in winter to meetings in Invermere or Cranbrook.

One summer we organized a meeting in our tiny local community of Boswell, in the ancient Quonset hut that served as the community hall. All the locals, young or old, came and made speeches. Even my father made a speech. And, for no particular reason that we ever figured out, soon after that the project was cancelled. But I always liked to think it had something to do with people like our neighbour, seventy year old, white haired Charlie Wilson, Alan's dad, standing and declaring, "Well, I'll lay down in front of them bulldozers myself if I have to, to stop this thing."

Now I looked at the fear in my son's eyes and I kept on reading and writing and talking to my friends. The more I thought about it the more absurd nuclear weapons became. I read Jonathan Schell's *The Fate of the Earth*. I signed up for peace newsletters and the more I read the more it seemed obvious that if enough people simply pointed out how ridiculous the whole notion of nuclear war is, well, of course, the government—which after all, was democratically elected—would listen, and then would change.

In 1985, there was a series of women's peace conferences leading up to an international conference in Nairobi organized by the United Nations. It seemed pretty impossible, given the tiny amounts of money Len and I were living on, but I decided to go to the women's conference in Halifax. I had no money at all for such a thing but, in those days, nothing much fazed me. I still had a lot of faith that if I wanted to do something badly enough, it was probably possible.

I saved some money and my friend Carol, now working as a dental hygienist, always faithful and loving, chipped in with enough to buy the $800 round trip ticket to Halifax. Len drove me to the airport. It was a strange feeling to walk away from my kids and Len and fly away. I somehow made it through the airport in Toronto and got on the right plane to Halifax. When I got off the plane there was a sign saying Halifax Women's Peace conference, which was great because I hadn't realized the Halifax airport was twenty miles out in the woods and I had no idea where the conference was.

When we went to get into the van the other women there introduced themselves and one who was blond and whose name I had heard on CBC radio looked at my ancient backpack—into which I had crammed my few good clothes—and said, "Oh, going camping?"

I couldn't think of anything to say. I might as well have had hayseeds in my hair. The other women were from Toronto and had smart luggage, great haircuts and beautiful suits.

When we got to the university we were shown to our rooms. I unpacked and stood by the window for a while, wondering what I was doing so far from the woods and so far from home. I thought of hiding in my room for the whole four days but I got hungry and went to find the cafeteria. It was full of women. I hesitated in the doorway, then wandered towards the food table. As I was standing in line, the woman ahead of me asked my name and where I was from. She was from Denman Island. She had read a piece I had written in some peace newsletter. When we sat down with our loaded plates, I was introduced to a whole group of women.

At some point in the conference I found myself sitting with some other women who had volunteered to write the statement from the conference that would be presented to the United Nations. We argued for about three hours and after everyone had gone to bed, I found a typewriter somewhere and wrote what I thought everyone had been saying. I left copies of it for the group to read.

When I staggered into breakfast the next morning, everyone stood up and cheered. That afternoon I stood and read the statement to the assembled group of five hundred women from around the world. The next morning, very early, I got back on a plane and flew home again, wondering just where I had been and what had been accomplished.

I went back to what I had been doing; I took small bits of time to write. I planted the garden and went for coffee and long walks with my mother and waited every day for the kids to come home from school.

There was a herd of elk living that winter on the other side of the river. Occasionally I could see them from the house, brown shadows moving slowly along the bank or disappearing into the wall of cottonwood and willow. One day I went down there to have a look. I went across the old railroad trestle and down the embankment to the sand. I had left the dogs at home.

The wind was blowing hard down the river and the elk couldn't smell me although they could see me coming. They watched me all the way down the bank until I was only a hundred feet from them. They trotted back and forth, sniffing the air and snorting at it, while I stood. I stood still and stared out at the river.

When they went back to grazing I moved each foot, one at a time, as slowly as I could, until I was about ten feet from them. By now they had decided I was probably nothing more interesting than a slow moving tree and had gone back to grazing on the dry yellow grass that grew out of the sandy mud, but they still weren't sure. They kept putting their heads up to look at me, moving closer and away, trying to get a definite scent, a sense of who or what I was. We danced slowly together, moving side by side. I stared at their delicate noses, their flickering ears, their round bright eyes. I was near them but not of them. I was also slightly terrified. I was conscious that they had large hoofs, long legs, that if they wanted to turn on me and stomp me into the ground, it was entirely possible for them to do so. I didn't think they would but, finally, the sense of trespass, of wrongness, was too much for me. I began to move backwards and away and they, who had been suspicious all along, now had their suspicions confirmed. They snorted indignantly at being fooled and trotted, hoofs clicking, into the trees and I went home.

That autumn my daughters graduated from high school and moved to Vancouver. I went off to Victoria for a Women and Writing workshop and, while I was there, I got a job in Edmonton, running a women's organization. Once again, I dragged my reluctant and unhappy family away with me. No one wanted to go to Edmonton. Our house was still unfinished. The boys were ensconced in school and busy with their friends and sports. But I was going quietly mad from loneliness, poverty, unemployment and ambition, and I was determined to change my life once again.

Chapter Ten

THREE YEARS LATER I got an offer to teach at a First Nations college in Merritt, BC. Len was studying nursing in Kamloops and I was working at the Women's Centre there. The time in Edmonton had left me emotionally scarred. The women's movement, from which I had learned so much and in which I placed so much love and hope and trust, was fragmenting, disintegrating amid accusations of racism, classism and political incorrectness. When I first got there I thought I had found an ideological paradise based on collectivity, love between and among women, caring for each other and changing the world. Three years later I had sat in a room and watched the organization, for which I had worked so hard, pull itself apart, everyone demanding that it go in a different direction.

Len had left Edmonton after the first year. He had decided he needed a new career direction as well and had enrolled in the nursing program at Cariboo College in Kamloops. When I finally left Edmonton I took the boys and went back to the log house. The girls were going to university in Vancouver. The boys and I spent a long and lonesome fall while I tried to come to terms with my disintegrating life. The job in Kamloops seemed like a lifesaver but I was tired of the women's movement, tired of feminism. Len was involved with school. The job at the First Nations college came as a relief.

I tried to remember what I knew or what I understood about First Nations people. Mostly I remembered Mabel's O'Neil's warm round face and riding wild horses and the night I ran away to live with the O'Neils. I had always identified with being something like an Indian; through my childhood reading I had cobbled together fragments of identity. The person I most wanted to be resembled a crazy quilt combination of Robin Hood, Annie Oakley, Huckleberry Finn and Cochise. There were all those childhood dreams of running away, of hiding in the woods. There was the wandering around with a hatchet, a 22 rifle and a can opener, heating my beans over the fire.

But I didn't know much about real Indians, other than what I had read; the standard Canadian and American history, sad stories of loss.

I hadn't taught much before either. In Edmonton I had taught writing in the University extension program and I had read lots of books about teaching writing and I thought I could invent the rest. After all, inventing and playing a role was still what I thought I did best.

So I wasn't sure what to expect when I started teaching at the First Nations college.

During the first class that fall, I thought maybe we could go out in the bright sun and have a storytelling session, get to know each other, practice the concept of storytelling. When I suggested it, people were hesitant. But, after a lot of fussing over the grasshoppers and whether the women would get grass stains and pine needles on their skirts, we settled down on a grassy knoll under a pine tree to tell stories about our lives. Three hours later, we were still there. We had used two boxes of Kleenex and I felt like my skin had been burnt off. My years of working in the women's movement hadn't prepared me for these stories. When we finished I went back to the campsite where I was staying until I could find a house. I wandered along the beach in the blazing sun, staring stupefied at the twisted, fire-varnished roots of ancient trees, lava rocks. Finally I went and lay in the water and let it float me away. I felt like I had been given a load of burning stones to carry. I let them sink to the bottom.

Over the next two years I tried to get used to horrific stories. Much as I loved the work and the people, I knew I wasn't going to be able to stay long. My uneasiness at being a white person standing at the front of a classroom of native people grew. I dutifully went to sweats when I was invited. A women's healing circle started meeting at my house. I sat on the beach below the beautiful cabin I had rented on Nicola Lake, tended the fire, the only white face, while women I worked with talked about their lives and wept in the light of the flames.

One day I went for lunch with my friend Sandra. She was a Tsimshian woman who had grown up in Port Simpson, north of Prince Rupert, but had gone away to school in Vancouver when she was twelve. She had started the healing circle that met at my house. We had banded together against the strange manipulations of the administration. I admired her immensely. She was beautiful, well educated, with an amazing instinct for figuring out what was really going on around her. We usually had fairly raucous lunches, a group of us would grab a table and then other people from the college would show up, students, colleagues and friends.

But today was different. The cafe was quiet when we came in. We ordered our food and sat down and then someone handed Sandra and I that day's edition of the Vancouver Sun. There had been a famous court case wending its way through the BC Supreme Court and now the judge had handed down his ruling in the case that has become known as Delgamuuk.

Judge McEachern's ruling was negative. He ruled that the Gitxsan Wet'suwet'en people didn't have title to their traditional lands. Silence descended over the small cafe as we all read the paper. Sandra began to cry. I sat there feeling stupid, wondering what to say and unable to think of anything. But gradually another feeling came wandering by, unexpected and confusing. It was a feeling of being a trespasser, an intruder. Politically I was aware of the issues involved but this was a feeling of something older, deeper and unbridgeable. It was the fact of our race and our history.

No matter how much I understood, and how much I sympathized, history stood between us. We could be friends in spite of it, allies even, we could understand each other but the facts of history are cold, implacable and unshakeable. We went back to work and continued our friendship but something had changed, something had awoken in me, questions I couldn't answer. I had always been so sure of my place in the world, of belonging to a particular place, a particular piece of land. I had thought that would give me commonality with First Nations people. So where did this sense of intrusion, of non-belonging, come from? And what should I do with it?

Sometime much later, I was walking along the beach by the lake with a group of students. For some obscure scheduling reason I was trying to teach an English class on Friday afternoons. Everyone else in the school packed up at noon and went home and I was desperate to try anything to keep people in class and keep their attention. But my inventiveness had limits. So today I had proposed we walk along the shore to the site of an old pit house. It wasn't far and it might give us something new to write about.

But it felt so odd, walking through the sun with people whose

Chapter Ten

ancestors had always lived here. Always. Whose ancestors might have built the pit house we were going to see. It wasn't that they knew any more about the place than I did. I had studied it, written about it, talked about it. But they knew it differently than me.

One woman remarked casually about having her grandmother's memories of where, on this particular hillside, to pick berries. Dust piled in my mouth. I wanted to lie down on the sand. No—more than that, I wanted to go home. I wanted to be at home, I wanted to find my home and belong there; no more wandering. If she had her grandmother's memories, what memories did I have? I had the O'Neils and the farm. I had wild horses tearing through my dreams, my grandmother's fingers tearing at my hair, trying to get the snarls out of it, her voice tearing at me, her condemnation of what I loved.

I knew I had stumbled over a central, crucial dilemma, not only in my life but in many people's lives. I had read what First Nations people had to say about the meaning and importance of the land in their lives. I had thought I understood it. Now I realized there were depths and layers of understanding that might not be accessible to me, however well-meaning and well behaved I was. I had sat in meetings with thoughtful ecologists and environmentalists and heard them use the term Mother Earth over and over without questioning. Now I began to wonder where this term had come from and if we really knew, as white people, what it meant. I had tried to talk about my attachment to the farm, to the Kootenays and to the lake to a few friends and had been met with polite incomprehension. When I said I didn't want to live anywhere else, that in fact, I wasn't capable of living anywhere else, people often looked at me skeptically. After all, I wasn't living there now. So what was I talking about?

When I first got the job in Merritt at the First Nations College, I tried commuting from Kamloops but it was too far. I rented a small cabin on the shores of Nicola Lake and spent the weekends with Len and the boys in Kamloops.

After they brought my stuff to the cabin and drove away, I walked in the door and was met with silence. I had never lived alone. I went to the Safeway in Merritt to buy groceries and wandered the shelves, unable to think of what I might want to eat. For over twenty years, I had cooked for other people and had eaten what I made for them. I had no idea what I actually liked to eat, apart from tea, popcorn and donuts.

In the evenings the silence in the cabin was deafening. I was so used to voices, the fridge door opening and closing, the stereo fighting with the television, kids complaining, fighting, talking, singing. To fill the silence I started another novel. I stared out the window at Nicola Lake, which, in the fall, was full of gold tints from the bright yellow of the poplars on the hills. In the morning, before I left for school, a family of beaver came by. A brilliant male loon lived in the bay. A pair of golden eagles lived in a pine tree up the hill. It wasn't Kootenay Lake but it was familiar.

Len graduated from nursing school and moved back to Creston. I didn't go with him. I sat by the window and kept on writing. But I was terrified that my family and my marriage were disintegrating and it was all my fault, my fault for working, my fault for being independent, my fault for wanting to write, my fault for not being at home where I belonged. I wrote to fill in the silence and keep away the guilt and the accusations. But silence and loneliness grew around me anyway.

When I arrived at the college I had been away from the farm for over five years, moving and working and trying desperately to stay connected to my family and my marriage. But I was still a patchwork person, full of dreams and ideas, still desperate to be a writer. Even though, by now, I had published a book of poems as well as lots of stories and journalism, I still hesitated to name myself writer, still

Chapter Ten

didn't feel part of any kind of writing fellowship, and still didn't know what I was doing with my life.

During my first day at the college, I met a woman who was just leaving. "This place is a glorified residential school," she said. I had no idea what she meant but, during my three years there, I began to get a glimpse of what she had meant.

I had spent my time at the college trying to figure out what was going on, trying to analyze the politics and find a place within a racial and political complexity. I had done what I knew how to do—I had read all the books I could get my hands on about First Nations people. I had read books about racism and the history of white and First Nations encounters. And I had tried to figure out what I was supposed to do.

And I had listened, and listened hard, to the women who met at my cabin, who sat around the fire on the beach below the cabin, while the black lake water lipped at the sand and I realized for the first time that I knew almost nothing of who I was in terms of being part of something, part of a family, part of a community, a tribe, a history, a people. I was amazed that I didn't know this. Where were the stories, I wondered, of the people who had left wherever they had left and come to Canada? Why, in a family that lived inside stories, didn't I know the stories and the history, even about my great grandparents? Who had they been? Why had they left wherever they had been? What stories had been lost? I needed to know.

After I left the college, I began looking for answers to the many questions about history and memory that my time there had engendered.

Eventually I found the history of my father's family, of the Borderers, Scottish Reivers, outlaws, a people with a darkly romantic history.

In particular, the Borderers were famous as riders, men and women whose lives, whose livelihood, depended on their horses.

I read that they lived by raiding their neighbours, riding their sturdy black horses.

I remembered galloping Lady to the top of the hill in the orchard, waving my sword. We didn't have television so where I got my models for the games of charging cavalry I played out in my head I'm not sure. They were like echoes of something far away and long forgotten. Lady carried those echoes for me and then I carried them away from the college, back to the farm, into the future and across the ocean.

I went with a friend to England and then to the border of Scotland. I felt like a combination of a foolish grinning tourist and an idiot child, journeying through England. I felt like I was living through my childhood– it wasn't England or the English I was seeing but stories and legends. I was living inside all those books.

When I told my hosts in Carlisle, in Cumbria in northern England, where I wanted to go, they laughed. "No one lives up there," they said. But that's where we went.

We drove past stonewalls and over arched stone bridges, into hills polka-dotted with tree plantations. We went through villages with brick and stone houses, past farms and sheep and hedges.

It was May and the slopes and hills were layered with daffodils, bending in the wind and the rain.

"Damn flowers," said the young man who had been coerced into driving me. "They're everywhere, bloody fools are always planting them, something to do with some poet."

We found the cemetery eventually, a rough patch of ground on a high hill, surrounded by rock walls and fields full of daffodils. There was barely a house in sight. The wind blew hard up the hill and rain fell in my face. I wandered from stone to stone, reading the inscriptions, so many Armstrongs about whom I knew nothing, except for bits and pieces of stories, legends and songs.

Chapter Ten

The young man who had driven me there stomped his feet and swore at the rain.

"Let's get back to England," he said, "back to civilization."

But I was sitting on the ground in the rain, smiling to myself. The wind blew up the hill towards me from the names of my reading, the names of the stories, from the Liddell Water, from Mangerton Farm, from Newcastleton, from the fells and dales and swamps of my history.

I sat on the grass. I listened to the rooks as they wheeled and shook the sky with their announcement that a stranger was here. I sat and sat without moving, without thinking. I was nothing. I was happy. I thought about those black horses and the people who had ridden them. I knew a little more about belonging, but not nearly enough.

Chapter Eleven

FINALLY I CAME HOME again to my parent's farm. The job at the college was clearly over. I had gotten into an unwinnable war with the administration. I had gone to the principal at the college with some of the stories of racism that I had heard from other First Nations students and staff. He announced that there was no racism or sexism at the college because the college's constitution forbade it. But I asked permission to organize an anti-racism workshop anyway. Everyone hated it and everyone felt hurt at the end. My friends from the women's circle had talked, had told their stories. The coordinators did the exercises they had developed to raise awareness. None of it worked. The workshop was summarized by one First Nations woman who was married to a white man. "We should just all try and be friends," she said.

After that the administration didn't fire me, they just made my work life untenable until I quit. I said goodbye to the beautiful cabin on Nicola Lake that had been my refuge for three years; I packed everything in my car and came home, once more, to the farm. The week after I got there, my mother picked up a saucepan and walked across the yard. She and my father moved into the new log house which my father had been intermittently building since I was a child. None of us had ever expected him to finish it but one day, magically, it was done. It was new. My mother, for the first time in her life, had new everything, a new stove, new fridge, new drapes, new dishwasher.

The old farm house, the house in which I had grown up and which my mother and father had once made homey and comfortable, was now mine, but it sulked after they left. I sat at night beside my computer, afraid to go to bed.

I loved the old house, but all our lives we had joked about it being haunted. When I first moved home, every evening the cat I had brought with me sat and stared down the hall, hissed and spat. I tiptoed down the hall and crawled into bed, tucked the blankets around me, hoping not to see any strange white shapes.

My mother had always loved to tell ghost stories. My children used to gather around her at night while she told them about Jimmy's ghost on the Mannarino place, or about the ghost that tried to smother her. She sat up in bed the next night with her Bible and it went away. One night, she said, she sat up in bed and saw an enormous cat with glowing green eyes sitting on the chair beside her. By the time she woke my father, the cat had flowed like smoke off the chair and away.

When my kids used to come home from Mom's to the trailer, they had to go by the place where my dad slaughtered chickens. They tiptoed by, then ran screaming, pursued by imaginary chicken ghosts.

Now the old house refused to let me in. Well, I had been hanging out with First Nations people. Had I learned anything? One night I lit sage and cedar and wandered through the house, asking for peace and harmony. The cat stopped hissing and I began sleeping better. I had some money from the Canada Council. I had finished a novel and sent it to a publisher. To my amazement, they accepted it. I started another.

Len lived down the road in our house. We had dinners and visits but there were too many shadows; we had managed to hurt each other too much by now to get past it all though we kept trying.

At the First Nations college there had been lots of talk about dysfunction, addiction and general fucked-upped-ness. One day I went to the counseling office, cleared off a shelf of self-help books and spent the weekend reading them, but nothing made much of an impression of me. Over the years, in the women's movement and in various other places, I had had a number of friends who talked about healing and other kinds of conversation that often seemed to suggest unhappiness was all a result of wrong thinking or some kind of wrong attitude. But my unhappiness, such as it was, had always seemed to me to be much more about being poor, about always having too much to do, about never having time to write, about being endlessly cold in the winter, and never being able to live the life I thought I wanted to live even though it seemed to me I had thrashed around in many directions trying to find it.

Len and I were still friends, still co-parents of the kids, but we couldn't talk to each other anymore. I missed him endlessly but I had also spent a long time thinking about how incredibly bad I was at relationships. One afternoon, in my cabin at Nicola Lake, I suddenly realized that I had never actually chosen to be in a relationship. I had fallen into them for all the wrong reasons, because I was scared or desperate, or confused. But I had never, since High School, really lived on my own. During the five years at the farm as a single mother, I had leaned hard on my parents and my friends to survive. And I never had five minutes to myself. Either I was working in the garden or I was with the kids.

Now I was still desperately poor but at least I had time to write. I made the discovery that most emerging writers make, writing doesn't pay much. After the Canada Council money ran out, I tried various ways to make money until finally I began driving to the college in Cranbrook—a round trip of 200 miles—once a week, to teach writing. From this I made $600 a month.

I loved the drive. Every year, the long fall blended into winter; the gold-tinged hills blended with the blue smoke from slash fires. I drove through a part of the county that was too cold and too high to be much good for farming; there were a lot of small discouraged looking places. Beside the Moyie River, an abandoned trailer bled pink-fading-to-yellow insulation out of its guts. I drove the long distance with Mozart or Pink Floyd wailing from the stereo. At night I slid back through a black tunnel, with giant trucks crashing through the slush, deer and elk peering from the frozen sidelines.

When I got home I'd build up the fire, crawl into bed, watch David Letterman for five minutes, lay there listening to the snow hissing against the windows, and fall instantly, gratefully, asleep, glad to be home, glad to be not driving anywhere for a while.

The old farmhouse had never had any insulation in the walls and, no matter how much wood I stuffed into the roaring furnace in the basement, it never really got warm. My father, by contrast, kept my mother, in the new house, in a state of near greenhouse warmth, and still she shivered at the slightest draft. Four or five times a day, when I was writing, I ran went over there to get warm and drink some more coffee.

A friend in Edmonton, who had started a small publishing company, asked me to write a children's book; not a genre I had considered before but I liked it once I got started. I wrote another novel, along with poems, essays. As often as I could, I threw brown envelopes into the green mailbox across the road and then went on

Chapter Eleven

with my life. I had no income at all from April to September other than what I could make off the farm but in summers the house filled up with people and somehow there was always food and wine and trips to the beach in the late afternoon. It was the life I once thought I wanted.

But the dark periods, the restlessness, the itch to go somewhere else, the poverty and the lack of recognition dragged at me. Winters were long. Some nights I stared into the darkness and drafted suicide notes as a kind of poetry.

After family dinners I came home wrapped in loneliness. I missed my kids, Len, working, money. Depressions settled into my bones like black ink.

I got up one muddy spring morning and squelched across the yard, as I did every morning, to drink coffee with my mother. This particular morning she looked at me and said, "You were such a happy child. What happened to you?" My mother always had a genius for poking a pointed question into the most sensitive place she could find. I didn't answer. All I wanted was a cup of coffee and a chance to get warm.

But, after I went back to my house, the question burrowed its way inside like a parasite and refused to go away.

I'd been writing all morning in scruffy clothes. I hadn't yet lit a fire in the ancient woodstove, so my house was freezing. No matter how hard I tried, I couldn't make enough money as a writer to live without a constant undertone of desperation about things like winter tires for my car or paying my always enormous phone bill.

I'd also been noticing lately that my mother had started writing everything down in a notebook. She'd write things like "fold laundry" or "bring peaches up from basement." She never talked about the notebook, just left it out on the table where she kept leafing through it. She wrote down all her grandchildren's birthdays, her sister's and brothers' birthdays. She wrote about music she liked and the names of programs on the radio but mostly she wrote down lists and lists of work.

My mother's sister had come to visit the summer before. She told us the same stories over and over. Then my mother had recently got word that she had been placed in a care home. Mom wouldn't accept this. "They've locked her up because they wanted her money," she said, over and over. I'd given up arguing and just nodded every time she told me this.

I drove into town that afternoon for a doctor's appointment. That spring of 1995. I couldn't seem to shake off an endless state of pain, stiffness and sore joints. Various doctors had looked at me, shaken their heads, shrugged their shoulders. I was pushing hard to finish a new book as well as keep up with the usual farm work. My niece was living with me part of the time and I was trying to tutor her through home schooling.

After the appointment, I parked in front of the restaurant where I usually had lunch, and went in and ordered tea. My friend Nora saw me and came in to have tea with me. "Oh, look," she said. "They're towing your car away."

I went back outside. The tow-truck guy was looking embarrassed. The parking ticket guy, whom everyone in town hated, said they were towing my truck because I had an unpaid parking ticket. Well, actually it was my son's ticket, but that didn't matter. I never paid parking tickets. I never could understand why should I pay to park on the side street of a town where there was never a shortage of parking. They didn't need my quarter. Or, considering the number of boarded up storefronts in town that year, maybe they did.

Small rural towns sometimes seem to me like spider webs spread on the landscape. They look friendly and welcoming, set in the middle of pretty scenery, of trees and mountains and green grass. But

Chapter Eleven

they trap people. This town and I had never had an easy relationship. It was a place where I had been refused jobs, a place where my kids had hated their school. But it was also a place I was used to, that I understood. It was hard to leave a place where even the guy towing my car away called me by name and mentioned that he went to school with my brother.

I pointed out to the parking ticket guy that I'd just come from my doctor and if I had to walk home and died it would be all his fault, but this made no impression on him. Finally I wrote a bad cheque for $45 to the tow-truck driver to get him to unhitch his shiny red tow-truck from my battered Honda and then I went back in to finish my tea with Nora.

"You know," she said reflectively, "when we were in high school, we all hated you. When you were stuck out in that little one-room school in Sirdar, our principal used to go on and on about you, about how you were so smart. By the time you showed up in high school, we were determined to get you."

I drank some more tea. Thirty years later, I thought, and the hell that had been high school could still get to me. But Nora was also one of the girls who had been, with her sister Eileen, one of my few pals in high school. We had been in the Drama Club together and we had kept our friendship after high school.

After Nora left, my friend Kaca came in and we had a late lunch. If I wanted, I could sit in the restaurant all day like this while people came in, visited and left. Then I'd stagger home soggy with tea and have popcorn for supper.

"I might move to Costa Rica," Kaca said, "or there's a job in Kazakhstan with an oil company I found online." I was jealous. Kazakhstan. That had to be more exciting than here.

"Isn't there a war on there?" I said.

"Maybe," she said, "but that's okay. They have camels and horses. I am sure I would love it." Kaca was little and skinny and had crawled out of Czechoslovakia while the Commies still had it. Another war and a few camels wouldn't faze her.

After I left the restaurant I bought $20 worth of groceries to get me through the week. The woman at the checkout counter in the grocery store said, "Are you writing another book?" I mumbled something.

"Well, you just keep writing them and I'll keep reading them," she said cheerfully.

I took my cheese slices and stoned wheat thins and went home. My dog came running, thrilled to see me; he was always thrilled to see me, simply because that was how he was made. Sometimes he was really irritating.

I got the fire going and the evening looked better. There was tea, popcorn, silence, solitude, books, the dog, the cat, the consolations of my writing life. When I got cold, I turned on a black-and-white TV, which I had bought at K-mart for $50 in 1974, which the kids used to watch in the trailer, then climbed into bed, under my blessed feather duvet. It was a present from my mother without which I would have long ago have been found, one morning, a frozen corpse. I huddled there with the pile of books and magazines I had brought home from the library in town, while the dog snored and farted beside me on the rug. And all night I tossed and turned. It felt like my body was burning up from the inside.

My parents' voices still resounded in my head. "Work or starve," my father had said. My mother would always sigh, "Time to hoist the anchor and get to work."

I had my father's attitude toward illness that if I ignored it, or worked harder, it would go away.

Once, years ago, I was ill with the flu. Being sick always sent me into a snarling rage, sent a trying-to-be-sympathetic Len away, silent. That was while we were homesteading, building the log house,

Chapter Eleven

clearing land, working, raising four kids. There was always too much to do. We worked from morning until night, fell into bed, got up in the morning, hit the ground running, did it all over again. We took our strength, our bodies' ability to keep up and keep going, for granted. There was no time, no space for illness.

My father often spent long winter days cutting trees for firewood and burning the branches. He claimed that working around a good big fire was a sure cure for most things. So I got up and staggered outside. I could barely walk. My head spun. I made it to the place where we had torn down an old shed and left a mess that needed cleaning.

I started a fire, dragged boards, branches, torn paneling to the fire, cursing and sweating, fighting my own weakness. The fire got taller and hotter, I sweated and fought some more and, gradually, as the afternoon passed, the yard got clean and I got well. It works: determination, peasant stubbornness.

At least, it used to work. But this time I went for weeks being sore and achy and exhausted. It was spring. The garden had to be planted, the flower-beds weeded, the lawn mowed, the fruit trees pruned. I kept up somehow, stumbling from task to task all day, falling into bed at night. But I was used to working through depression. It was one of the ways I had survived so far.

One day I decided, as a way of finally curing myself, to mow the whole damned lawn, about half an acre of rocks, logs, bumps, dog bones, weeds and some grass. I shoved the ancient lawn mower around and around, sitting down often and then getting up to keep going. It was crucially important to keep going. When I finished and went inside, I could barely move. I decided a hot bath would help. (That was when I could still get into a bathtub.) It didn't. When I crawled out, I felt like my body was on fire. I was freezing and burning at the same time. I took six Aspirin with codeine, wrapped a blanket around myself and sat over an electric heater shaking, my teeth chattering. I kept fading in and out of things. Finally I warmed up enough to go to bed. This time ignoring being sick wasn't working.

My parents were living on their pensions and what they could make off the farm. Money from the farm had slowly dried up. Once they had sold eggs and milk and butter, fruit and vegetables. But those markets had gone. Now they were struggling to pay the taxes on the farm and there wasn't much I could do to help.

My brother and father had logged the farm and my mother decided that my brother owed them money, so now every morning my mother said, "What are you going to do about your brother?" I dreaded this question.

"Mom, if you're so upset, talk to Bill, or call a lawyer," I'd say. It was our morning ritual.

"Oh, your father wouldn't like that," she'd say. "Your father doesn't trust lawyers. If your father would only talk to him. Can't you get your father to talk to him?"

"Mom, he doesn't listen to me. I'm not a boy. I don't have a chain saw. I don't kill things."

"Well, we'll just have to sell the farm," she'd say. "We don't have any choice. We have to sell something." Nobody wanted to sell the farm, least of all my mother. I'd usually try to turn the conversation to something else, something cheerful.

Most afternoons in the winter my mother and I would walk to the beach. We would look at the water and clouds, say nothing, and then come home to tea with the winter darkness setting in and conversation about what each of us was cooking for supper. Every Thursday, we drove to church and back for choir practice. Our conversations ran endlessly in the same ruts, the kids, the farm, my dad, my brother, and what to have for tea.

Now that she had brought it up, I found myself trying hard to remember what really did go on when I was a child. In my mother's stories, my childhood somehow had become this marvelous magic documentary, fruit hanging on trees and days spent fishing, wandering the mountains with my horse, or picking wild strawberries.

Then there was the other story, the one I had told assorted friends and lovers, about the endless work, my bitter critical father, my crabby siblings, my oh-so-poor, oh-so-sad mother, who told me once I just had to learn to manipulate men if I wanted to get anywhere. They were both true, like the two faces of Janus. It all depended on which truth I wanted to look at.

Now the farm seemed to split along these same lines as well; it became the sad farm, the funny farm, the place that broke my heart every time I looked at it, the place that held my life the way a mirror holds light or a glass bowl holds water. My border collie, Kin, and I walked to the beach every morning, the same semi-circle of brown sand, framed by round granite loaves of rock. Bone Bay, we had named it one summer, because a dead cow had washed up there. The O'Neil kids said they were human bones, ghost bones. It was the ghost beach.

One spring afternoon Kin and I set out, he carrying his newly found soccer ball, long buried under the snow that was finally disappearing. The Delicious tree by the garden was full of robins; the garden a river of mud littered with islands of snow. Occasionally one of the robins would fly down to pick through the mud. The yard was a patchwork of dead leaves, snow, ashes and sawdust. Snow melting off the roof in huge crashing chunks had crushed the honeysuckle and the clematis. The potentilla and other shrubs were also flattened. Spring was always black and grey, sharp edges, black branches like dead hair on the fruit trees.

We went down the hill, across the orchard, over the rocks and onto the granite sand. Mist hung over the lake. Kin worried the soccer ball until I kicked it into the icy water and he crashed in after it. The lake was low, the water still. A sucker hung motionless, just under the surface of the bay. Fungus whitened its tail.

Rain began to dimple the water as we left the beach. When I looked closely I could see, just under the mat of mud and dead grass, green sprouting already, beginning the mad growth that would swell into abundance through the summer and fall. By the driveway, tiny spikes of daffodils punched the soil's surface.

The next morning I spilled tea on my computer and it spluttered and died. When I went to my mother's house I listened to her litany about selling the farm. I wanted her back, the warm laughing mother I once had, but now there was no room in her thoughts for me. Everything was a potential disaster, even the flowers coming and the snow going. There was nothing now in which fear didn't loom for her. More and more I avoided this litany, changed the subject, tried to be jolly, humour her out of it.

But that morning I was the one needing comfort. When the dog finally talked me into it I left for our walk, with my head down, sullen, deliberately trying to notice nothing. But at the beach, the light from the water pulled my head up. There, as always, was the timeless unchanging face of Castle Mountain. I was so temporary, walking through this ancient geology, the granite shell on which my feet banged and thudded. Against this, the chaos in my life realigned into being less important but it still didn't go away.

I was suspended in time, waiting for tomorrow and my computer to be fixed, hung out between mountains, waiting. The radio had predicted more snow.

Some days all my friends and I talked about was weather. It would have been funny if the weather weren't so pervasive, inside and out. As I came back to the house I thought about how exhausted I was that spring, an exhaustion made savage by the mess and frantic thought of the coming summer season, five months with no salary, still the same painful weakness in my joints and muscles, and so much work to do. I shut the rage away, went in my house and got ready to drive to writing class.

After I came home from the class I walked to the orchard. It was after eleven but still light enough to see; there was a crescent moon hanging over the lake. A flock of geese went by high up on the mountainside. They reminded me of women crowded together, talking, talking, sharing gossip and information and how are you doing and oh my sore wing and wasn't that last bit of marsh grass just delicious. I didn't know what they were talking about and I didn't know why as a human I responded so nostalgically to their gabble; perhaps because it was high and free and they were all together and I was alone. The lake was still. The sky was still faintly pink.

Who loves this place, I said? Who or what in me is so connected here? Who loves this flooded lake, this still night, these crazy geese? Why can't I leave?

I had committed myself to the idea of land when I was a child, I thought. It was love that committed me, love and beauty. I had been trying to find a language for it ever since. The animal in me knew what it loved, where it lived, what it was attuned to. Some animals, like cats, hate travel. Some, like horses, can adjust to it but mope. Some are gypsies. But all have homes, ecosystems, places they live. I have no answers. I only knew that to which my whole being responded.

The year wore on. My siblings and I barely talked. We avoided one another. I began to dream about leaving the farm but I needed somewhere to go and something to do. I had needed a master's degree for a long time. Maybe with a master's degree I could get a better teaching job. I sent off an application to the University of

British Columbia Creative Writing Department.

One day in late June, Kin and I set off to look for wild strawberries. There had been both rain and sun and the air billowed with the scent of wild roses; many coloured irises bloomed in my gardens.

I was always greedy for wild strawberries, the first fruits of the season; it's hard and satisfying work to get even a mouthful. My brother and I always used to hunt wild strawberries together when we were kids. It was one of the things we shared and loved and never talked about.

While I was hunting I kept thinking about the small shabby house in a southern US city where I lived with Herb. The yard there was bare and bleak and I had tried to dig it up and plant some flowers. I remembered my husband coming home one day and standing in the yard with another man. I watched their feet shift back and forth on the newly sprouted flowers as they talked, until there was nothing left but flattened ground.

My brother worked incredibly hard. He and his partner, Claire, had bought a house next to the farm and rebuilt it. Every morning I would hear his diesel truck clatter out of the yard at six and I would roll over and go back to sleep. He made a lot of money cutting down trees.

When I was a child, I didn't mind watching as my father shot and butchered cows and pigs and chickens. I never questioned my father's dexterity with a chain saw and giant machines. I could hardly wait to get a chain saw of my own. I liked helping to butcher. Now, so much later, I only wanted to walk through life like I walked through the woods, quietly as a shadow, disturbing nothing and watching where I put my feet.

I went away through the woods next to the farm admiring the finely tangled mat of driftwood along the lakeshore, the cold brown

Chapter Eleven

water lapping back at heights everyone thought it had been dammed away from. The dogs flushed a grouse right in front of me. She fluttered her wings and screeched; her tiny chicks scooted for a hole in the ground. When they were safe she flew into a tree and clucked her indignation. I passed by as quickly as I could, calling the dogs to come away and let her be.

One day in early July I went swimming for the first time that year. I stood at the water's edge. Rain was slanting down on the other side of the lake but the sun shone on me. The mountains were massive, dark green and blue in the slanted varying light.

I shed my clothes, waded into the water. It was warm at the edge and ice cold further out. I let it take my breath and kept swimming. I swam to the rocks circling the bay, hauled myself out and lay there for a while. It hurt but not too badly. There were no boats on the lake because of the storm. I sat there in the warm wind until I couldn't stand it anymore and slid back in the water and swam some more. I wanted to be in and under and full of the lake, full of summer and strawberries and the heat coming and the storm waiting on the other side of the lake and the mosquitoes hovering at the shore. I swam and gasped and remembered all over again the sensual intimacy of swimming, like making love, slow rolling and rolling in the water.

I came out of the water and leaned against the sun-heated rock. The kids used to warm themselves on these rocks. They claimed when they listened closely they could hear voices. I listened but I didn't hear anything from inside the rock. But it is true, sometimes the rocks hum; maybe it's insects or wind but they hum. I used to listen to them. They hummed and they danced in late afternoon the reflections from the water.

I could live anywhere. I could love anyplace. That's what I tried to tell myself. It's the utter familiarity of this place that translates into profundity. It's the same lake and the same beach and the same summer repeating itself like an ancient liturgical chant. Before I got sick I used to swim out for half a mile into the lake, over the depths of black green water, and lie and bask and roll, spouting and playing like a demented goofy whale. The water always feels safe. It holds me up, licks me clean. I am its plaything as it is mine.

I rubbed my back against the rock. My scalp tingled from the cold and my skin was as soft and clean as a washed leaf. I finally left and floated up the hill, stopped at the garden for strawberries, a new cauliflower, onions and garlic, the first perfect raspberry and even a few half ripe Saskatoons. It was the grazing time of year, when the earth dripped with food. I found myself wandering through the garden, endlessly nibbling, a satisfied herbivore.

After dinner the college phoned. They had promised me two writing courses next winter. Two courses meant the difference between desperation and comfort, between fixing the car and continuing to drive with no brakes, between buying wood and scrounging it, between fear and coping. Now they wanted me to teach the course as one course, the second class simultaneously by videoconferencing. I would only get paid for one class. It wouldn't save them any money. The money they saved in not paying me would go to pay for the technology.

I needed enough money to survive another winter, needed enough for snow tires, car, wood, electricity and my huge phone bill. I needed to catch up a bit. But these were bureaucrats dealing with budgets. What did my bald tires mean to them?

I went to Wilson's to watch the sunset from their deck. We sat in their screen tent to avoid the mosquitoes. I felt bowed down by other people's troubles. My friend Carolyn had been phoning every day because her mother had been re-diagnosed with cancer. My friend Mary's five months pregnant daughter-in-law had malignant melanoma. My mother wanted a family conference talk about selling the farm. I'd sooner have been put through torture.

The next day my friend Juanita and I spent a day picking

strawberries and black currants. Over lunch we discussed how much our community had changed, how we felt it slipping away. Once rural community was a network of taken for granted obligations. I learned from my parents that one gave whatever one had; friends and neighbours always went away loaded with whatever surplus we had. I learned the odd and wonderful lesson that the best way to manage the rural balance sheet was to give and give and give, with the assurance that, in small and subtle ways, it would always come back. But those values were disappearing. Our wealthy new neighbours had ingested the idea of winning, of always getting the best of a bargain, of the sense that money is the only arbiter of value. But rural community isn't about winning, it's about sharing and survival.

Before she left we wandered with our teacups among the flowers, peering at the combination of neon lychnis, pastel foxgloves and glowing white delphiniums, discussing colour and texture. That afternoon, after she left, the yellow lilies opened.

My father had always hated weeds. Gardening is an endless battle against weeds but of course weeds are mostly flowers. He had spent years cutting down and poisoning buttercups and daisies and dandelions, He conceived a special hatred for curly dock. Maybe he was onto something. Maybe they really were out to take over. After all, he was running out of time, but flowers and weeds have all the time and persistence in the world. The irony was that, like most other people in the Kootenays, he had gotten interested in herbs and self-medicating himself, and he had begun drinking his own peculiar herb tea mixture every night and lecturing the rest of us about doing the same.

My friendships in the Kootenays are long ones. Conversations with my friends are variants on the same themes we have been pursuing over the course of thirty years of friendship. We used to talk with babies on our laps, sugar and tea puddled on the table, the older kids running in and out the door. Now our lives are neater, quieter, but other cracks are showing up. All of us have lived our lives as rural women. Carol came from the city, Joan from England via a small town; we've been neighbours and friends, our kids have grown up together. We have always all lived as pivotal members of our extended families, parents next door, kids in and out as they got their lives together, went to school or came back for summer work. Now emotional pain seemed to be eating up what we thought would be the serenity of these years. Joan's daughter had left home in anger; Carol was worried about her youngest son. Joan and I talked about the pain in our families; Carol and I talked about love and illusion and enlightenment. We were all coping with loss: Joan's mother had died of cancer last year, Carol was working to keep her marriage together, I had the farm and my worry about my mother.

When I came home from Wilson's, the mosquitoes pursued me to the door. Mosquitoes made our summer like winter; we hesitated to go outside, we wrapped up in scarves, jackets and thick socks. They didn't last that long but they ruled our lives while they did.

Last night I had said to Alan that I might grow another garden next year...if there was a next year. The farm felt as if something, some spirit that used to animate us all, had left. We didn't talk anymore, my family and I. We were angry with each other but we didn't want to fight. We all retreated into silence. For a year I didn't talk to my father or brother. We turned our faces from each other. I spent my time reading Buddhist books in a search for comfort and understanding.

I sat every morning, in my flower filled, bird-song filled, peaceful porch, and read the commentaries of the Dalai Lama. Compassion, says the Dalai Lama, is the most important thing. But I could slide from compassion to anger and bitterness and back again in the blink of an eye. Contradiction must be part of the path to enlightenment.

Chapter Eleven

Contradiction seemed to be the twisted roots of my life here. Poverty and abundance. Love and bitterness. Spirituality and hillbilly squalor.

On July afternoons my mother and I picked the strawberries together. Soon we would be drowning in the abundance of summer.

One July afternoon the mosquitoes and I worked quietly away, me hoeing tomatoes, while a soft gray rain fell on our heads. Mosquitoes don't hurt. They just quietly drive you mad until, a million tiny pin pricks later, you run to the house, shuddering. All my life I have wondered how the animals endure it; not just mosquitoes but blackflies and deerflies and horseflies, and no shelter.

The gray afternoon wore on. There was a lid over me, over the valley. Nothing will ever happen, I thought. Up on the mountain, the ravens called and called with monotonous creakiness.

And then two real estate dealers showed up to measure my house. I didn't know they were coming. I told them to go away. When I tried to think of moving, I went blank. That morning a magazine had come with a picture of Vancouver on the cover. I loved to visit the city, to play there. My children were there. I could probably work there. I could buy things. What made it so impossible to imagine a life there?

When I was a child I would stare up at Castle Mountain, the broad-shouldered peak directly across the lake from the beach. It had a personality, something like what I imagined God to be, immensely old, imposing, lonely, terrifying and fierce. When I got older and went away to university, to the city, to marriage, the unchanging eternal face of the mountains became my touchstone.

That summer went by in a rush, a blur of kids and visitors and gardening and swimming and long leisurely suppers.

In September, I came home from a visit to Edmonton to a woodshed full of wood, thanks to my sons, to peace and silence and a terrible feeling of unease. All night, on the first night home, I lay awake, exhausted and unable to sleep. Usually the house folded itself around me like a warm and welcoming blanket, but something was uneasy, myself or the house, I'm not sure, and I only slept when morning began to come.

The unease began coming back from the airport. Driving by Moyie Lake the water was perfectly mirror calm, only dented with the small circles of trout rolling. Coming down through the twilight the newly golden trees were shining dim around the edge of the black lake. If only it was all so peaceful, if only this golden surface was the only truth I knew about this place. Coming back into my life, here after even a brief time away, was always like struggling back into clothes that didn't fit anymore. The place I escaped to, the only place that had ever fit, was my writing; it was a lonely but clear place. There was just me and the struggle to put words on paper and, through that struggle, to achieve something, some understanding, some clarity, something memorable.

"Are you still writing?" people in town would ask me over and over, mystified at my odd and obsessive hobby.

When I came home I went to the beach for a long while and sat in the sun. The impossibly dreamy beauty of September blazed all around me, the smoky haze on the gold tipped mountains, the clear water, the sky I could fall into, lie back on the sand and fall and fall until I was only a speck among the golden stars.

The farm was temporarily at peace. The real estate agents had gone away. My father had left me at the airport with a bitter retort about the farm being a millstone around his neck. I had said nothing. I had gotten on the plane and flown away. I had gone to bookstores in Saskatoon, Calgary and Edmonton, read from my books, and pretended to be a real writer for a week or so before coming home to the silence.

Chopping wood that winter was an exercise in torture as my arthritic hands swelled and curled into claws. I lay in bed at night feeling like my muscles were on fire from the inside. I had no energy left. It was hard to travel, hard to think, hard to work. When I arrived at the college to teach, it took me several minutes to get out of the car and straighten up. More and more I retreated into small pleasures and comforts, fire, a good dinner, a movie to watch later, some writing done, phone calls from friends.

Still I would go to bed with my head buzzing, ideas for new poems, the second part of the novel, bit and pieces of writing.

I wondered why the word *lonely* has such a sad ring to it. Perhaps lonely is different than alone, but they are also inextricably connected. I always thought that being alone in a crowd of people was far more difficult than going to bed by myself, with the dog, the cat, the pile of books and magazines that always littered the side of the bed. Loneliness was my drug, my consolation prize, the sweetness that flavoured the long hours at the computer, the companion that lurked on the path up the mountain or down through the garden. When I picked the last of the corn and peaches that summer, I wanted others with whom to share a sense of completeness. There should have been songs, there should have been a harvest festival, there should have been others lifting and carrying buckets of peaches alongside me. But there wasn't. There was me and the peaches and the land.

That fall I had picked the apples and grapes and pears and planted a combination of blue and gold tulips in the garden. I carried in huge bulging bellies of blue and green Hubbard squash, fifty pounds or more each, enough to feed an army of kids through the winter... if we still had an army of kids.

The peace continued that fall. My mother seemed better and I was writing, working on a couple of books at once. It was a fall of rain alternating with sun. In the sun, the lake turned that deep royal blue it only gets in late fall and early spring. Even if I were deprived of my ability to see anything but the light, I would know the changing seasons by the quality of the light. It starts to change in late August, the first days of sliding towards fall, to sleepiness and nostalgia and harvest.

My mother and I and my friends always turned inward during the winter. From November until February we barely saw the sun down in the bottom of the valley. A layer of cloud, smoke and the dust from the sand and ice covered roads covered the valley every winter. I tried to turn this to my advantage, by burrowing deeper within, by writing harder and longer.

I always liked the way animals stand in the winter cold, perfectly still, pulled into themselves. If you come near, they move away slowly, like fish drifting in water. They stand still, enclosed hidden furnaces, burning dried grass and crushed seeds, steaming away like dark furry kettles.

January has always been my least favourite month of the year. That January, warmth descended far into the depths of the earth. Nothing came in the mail but bills. Money had almost disappeared from my life. I was taking yet another magic remedy for arthritis. I couldn't remember what it was like to get up in the morning feeling well, to go down the steep basement stairs, chop kindling without wincing, throw logs on the fire, split knotty blocks of fir, go outside and prune apple trees, go riding, all the things I had once done with ease.

My mother seemed more and more fragile everyday. As a way of dealing with his worry, my father began to tell me stories of his childhood, his tone insistent, desperate. They were stories I'd heard before but now he told them as if there was something important in them I didn't understand, something I had to learn.

But we were now a family with a story. Once our story was that we were self sufficient, we worked hard, we grew our own food, we were tough as nails, we gave no quarter to anyone, we ignored the foolish suburban summer people. We were a family with land, a mini kingdom.

Chapter Eleven

It was all work, work and survive, survive and no room for useless things. What had held us together was our land and our sense of connection to it. Or maybe that was my story and my story alone. Connection is so easily something else; a bond is a chain, work is either glory or slavery. Maybe my brothers' and my sister's stories were those of bondage and slavery. I didn't know anymore.

One day I came home from town where I'd gone shopping and picked up the mail. It had poured rain all day and the evening was coming fast and dark. I was crawling back out of the hole into which a bland official letter from four days earlier—telling me I didn't get a grant—had sent me tumbling, a hole filled with an acid sense of failure so bitter and intense that it burned my skin, shriveled my soul back down into its very core. I put myself to sleep dreaming of suicide, I woke to the same comforting dream. I couldn't help but imagine the freedom from worry the money would have bought me. The impersonal cruelty of it was beyond dealing with.

"Don't take it personally," is the first thing every writer has to learn about rejection, but how to do otherwise? Ever since I was a kid, I have reacted to pain by fighting back; if I fell off my horse or my bike my reaction was furious, instinctive, instant, to get back on and conquer whatever it was that had thrown me. But I couldn't fight impersonal bureaucrats from far away who didn't give reasons for their decisions and who never had to know the reality of what they had or hadn't done.

So I did what I always do, what I knew best, split myself into a person shivering with anguish and despair and the other one, who got up, got dressed, went to town, taught a class, smiled and made conversation and drove the car home without sliding on the ice or hitting the deer which improvidently crossed my path on the Wynndel hill.

I arrived home to the comfort of a clean house, silence, tea, a New Yorker review of George Orwell's new collected writings and, finally, supper. I made a lovely supper out of popcorn, toast and oranges. I phoned Juanita after supper and we reflected on the joys of our separate solitudes, in our winter houses, in the dark evening rain, the joys of uninterrupted reading, of hot baths. Being alone was the only time I was not in a small agony of self-consciousness. Perhaps solitude is, for some people anyway, a necessary kind of existence. Why isn't it more celebrated? There is much joy in it, much joy in simple pleasures, in being able to notice them. Are there things you can't learn, can't know, can't remember to recognize, in company? If I were in a relationship, would I forget to notice the intense pleasure of silence, of reading, of my bed, of long walks alone, of coming in after walks? Of course, I have Kin. He doesn't ask much. Walks, food, his couch. He likes solitude too.

After supper I opened the mail. I had been accepted into the UBC Creative Writing Master's degree program. I had no money to go. But if there was one thing I was good at, it was coping without money. I would go and hope for some kind of miracle.

After supper, Kin and I went on our evening walk to the beach. The mountains stood there the way they always did, pointing their shadows down into the heart of the black and glossy lake. I kicked the soccer ball into the water for the dog to fetch but it got trapped on the edge of a mat of driftwood that had clogged the small bay.

It took both of us a while to get the ball back—me poking and prodding at the logs to get them loose, him scrambling from log to log as they rolled and sank under him. I got out on the raft of logs as well. It was hard to see in the evening light. The water sucked at the logs with its many mouths. I got away but left a shoe as a gift. The dog and I were both soaked and tired when we got the ball back and he held it triumphantly in his mouth all the way up the hill.

We felt pretty good about ourselves as we strolled through the early spring twilight. Geese babbled nonsense overhead and the smell of warming earth rose up from under my feet, which meant it was probably time to plant something or other. Tomorrow I would phone my kids. Tomorrow I'd start working on a new book.

After I decided to move away from the farm again, I needed money so I went to work in Edmonton, doing some editing for a friend. When I finished working in Edmonton, I drove down through Calgary, stopped in Fort Macleod, on to the foothills, through the Rockies to the Kootenays.

I had been living in other people's houses, living other people's lives for the past few months, working and trying to make money to go to school. I was tired of smiling, getting up at odd hours, eating breakfast when I didn't feel like it, hanging up my wet towels, stopping at two glasses of wine.

Now I was so tired of traveling that every place I saw, I imagined stopping, finding a place, a house, and simply staying there, having a life of my own. And each life would be in its own kind of place; in Northern Alberta, it would be among the poplar and aspen and cottonwood, the gruff farmers, oil wells and hydrogen sulphide flares, flat stretches of brush and sly greedy trees busily reclaiming any unplowed land.

I wanted to stop in Peigan country, near Brocket, where someone had spray painted a sign saying, Free Nation, No Treaty Indians. Two men were standing beside a fence post and tractor, stretching wire. The wind was blowing hard, hard, out of the Crowsnest. The horses stood with their heads down and rumps pointing to the mountains.

Or down through the other side of the Crowsnest; maybe I could live in Fernie, I thought, and never go skiing. I could have a little house on the dark mountains among the elk and moose and hunters in the fall. I could live alone, in all that snow. I kept thinking of my favourite Adrienne Rich poem about driving across the country, through towns she might have lived and died in, lonely.

And then I thought of the farm, a place I had lived all my life, and how perfectly and peculiarly lonely it was there, among the people I have known all my life. It's writing that made me lonely. It's all writing's fault, I thought. Writing made me an exile the first time I picked up a pen when I was six. Maybe I could quit writing and buy an RV, I thought, and understood that fantasy for the first time too. Oh, I knew so much about everything when I was driving. I imagined myself freewheeling it alone up the Dempster Highway to the Arctic Ocean and standing there, looking at the blue-black ice on the wild ocean.

I would have my dog for company. I'd never have to get out of the RV except to go for long windswept walks beside the Arctic. These days, they even have drive in bank machines. I could have a computer and a satellite dish and a wide screen TV.

Of course, I'd have to have some money but that wasn't today's problem. Just tomorrow's, when I got home and stopped being tragic on a windswept highway heading out of Alberta and had to get ready to move again out of the place that holds my life.

I have always wanted to write when I was driving. When I was a little kid, I liked to ride around in the back seat of cars because I could dream there. I didn't get to do it much because we had a pickup. Four kids and two adults in the front seat of a '57 Dodge didn't leave much room for dreaming.

The day before I moved away to go to UBC, my son and I were driving the lake road with his son, my grandson, asleep in the back seat.

"Do you think your grandmother has Alzheimer's?" I asked. I was driving so I didn't have to look at him.

"She's fine," he said. "You worry too much."

Chapter Eleven

The steering wheel shook because the tires were going bald. I never know what to do about tires. They're never just right for the time of year. Someone always tells me, "Oh, you shouldn't have your winters on now," or then they say, "Better get some new winter tires." It has worn me out over the years, worrying about tires.

"Should I get some new tires?" I asked.

"The tires are fine," he said.

"She phoned over to my house last week. She said she couldn't remember how to make biscuits."

Oh, c'mon, I had said. Of course you know how to make biscuits.

I wanted to say, "Do you think she'll die while I'm gone, do you think she'll fade away and forget everything?" but it was such a beautiful day, the road like a carved edge between the cliff and the bright blue lake.

"She's fine," he said again.

We drove on and on, balancing on the yellow line, the delicate and multicoloured exhaust trailing behind us in the cold fall air.

Chapter Twelve

I NEVER UNDERSTOOD BEFORE that memories are also a place to live. Now that I live at the farm again, Kin and I still always go for a last walk before bed. Usually we go to the beach. Sometimes we wander the old Hog Pasture, which hasn't been a hog pasture for sixty years. It's now owned by other people, has huge new houses on it that nobody lives in, both for sale. I'm trespassing but there's no one to see or care.

Plus I have some rights here. Or my memories do. And some needs as well.

Kin takes off, disappears into the darkness, running fast, nose to the ground. I depend on him to warn me about bears or cougars, but I'm not really nervous. Any self-respecting bear or cougar would hear me fumbling along and get himself as far out of the way as possible.

I'm never sure what I'm doing out here, tracing paths that only existed when I was a kid, paths that are now lawns and driveways. Still, I know the way, even in the dark. Over this particular path I went every day after school to fetch Tiny, the Jersey milk cow with the huge doleful eyes. She used to hear me coming and hide in the brush. I had to stand very still and listen until the occasional faint clank from her cowbell would give her away. Once I found her, she'd grudgingly head for the barn, her calf, her evening feed of grain and hay. I'd wander behind, a stick in my hand, which I didn't need, switching the clusters of snowberries off the bushes or the last dried elderberries from out of the thicket.

I'm glad to see that the same elderberry bush I used to walk by is still there. Elderberries are hard to kill. Maybe the new owner got tired of chopping it down, finally let it be and curved his driveway to go around it. An old European legend says that witches live in elderberry bushes. If you chop one down, the witch will curse you.

White people haven't lived long enough in this country to have similar legends. We don't know or believe anything about the spirits of the land. We don't think there are any. Maybe we believe that to our peril.

All my life I have watched people move in around me, chop down the trees, build driveways and houses and septic tank fields and lawns and gardens. Gradually they have built places that hold other memories, not mine. But these two houses are for sale because the people who built them are both dead and their children live far away and don't want to come here.

My memories are of these places before they were owned, civilized, tamed. Mine are of the old paths, the deer trails, the moss-beds under the spruce, the snowberry jungle with the secret swamp at its centre. Mine are a child's memories—it is my childhood I am prowling through out here in the dark, feeling my way over paths that my feet remember, that would be hidden to me by daylight.

I have an odd fantasy that I can see the paths, that the layers of feet—mine, the dogs, the cows, the O'Neil's crazy wild horses, deer and bears and skunks and other animals prowling the dark—have left thin molecular traces of themselves, traces that shine dimly in the night. What is probably true is that the paths are a hidden unevenness in the ground, that they refract the little available light—from the stars or a distant yard light—differently, and so maybe it is true that I can see them.

But I like my fantasy better, that the path is visible to me at night in the same way as the smells of wild animals are visible to the dog's questing nose—that it shines in some way I don't understand, that it is available to my seeking feet.

The paths remain—and the names. The names remain within our family; I don't know if the neighbours with their new houses have any idea that they now live in Sawdust Bay, Haley's Pasture, the Hog Pasture, or Bone Bay. These were the farm names, acquired easily, lost just as easily. Sawdust Bay still has thick piles of sawdust layered over with pine needles where Pierre Longueval milled out the lumber for his house and barns and chicken sheds, Haley's Pasture is where one of the first white men into the country trailed a herd of goats over the mountains, built four log cabins whose ancient bones still crouch under the fir trees. Someone has put a trailer on Pierre's sawdust piles; someone has built a driveway over the rock walls and rusty barbed wire Haley used for his goat pasture.

When I am home, I prowl the old paths remembering stories stored in the ground and waiting for me, shining up at me in the starlight. I prowl these paths looking for comfort, for roots, for balance, for reconnection. I know what I am really doing is wandering through my own history, looking for the next book, the new path, the next step on the road. When I lie in bed at night the paths still shine in my head. All night I walk their secret ways, at home and content.

When I need company, or just to catch up on the gossip, I drive down the road to the Sirdar Pub, where there's always good food and music and someone to talk to. Once, some years ago, the new owner of the pub in Sirdar got a new sign. As we drove down the long hill into Sirdar, the blurry, badly painted B looked like a D so many began to call it the Pud. Some of us still do that but new people don't get the joke because the sign has been changed.

Now when I sit in the Sirdar Pub, I stare across the tracks to the blank field that once was our school ground. One train still comes by each evening and, when it does, everyone yells Train. The waitress picks a number and we all look under our seats. The right number wins a free shooter.

The Sirdar Pub is where Alan Wilson and I went for dinner a month before he died. By then he was almost completely paralyzed by a brain tumour but we ate fried chicken and talked about the things we always talked about, about the lake and the weather and our kids and what the hell was with the CBC.

When I was struggling to become a writer, I would go to Alan and Joan's house at least two or three times a week for coffee. I'd come in the door, sit at the dining room table, leaf through their collection of magazines while Joan ground coffee beans.

Alan would see my truck and come up from the workshop where he was sandblasting the handmade gravestones he made. We'd drink our coffee and exchange whatever new gossip we had and talk about what we loved and hated on CBC radio which we listened to all day long while we worked.

The Sirdar Pub is where we went for dinner one night when my son and Joan and Alan's daughter were both working there. Marisa went into labour that night and Alan's first grandson was born. A month later, so was mine.

The stuffed fish and deer heads that were on the wall when I was eighteen and went for my first legal beer are still there, 35 years later. On warm summer nights when the mosquitoes gather in clouds around the windows, every new person enters to a chorus of "Quick, shut the door."

Chapter Twelve

As we ate dinner, outside clouds of smoke and a chorus of slaps rose from the new young people, the smokers, huddled together for protection near the back door by the kitchen.

Once, not long before Alan died, he and I were talking about Sirdar School and I couldn't remember the name of Mrs. Hare's dog that came to school with her every day and slept under her desk. When Alan and Santo and I were in Grade 7, the school was down to 8 students. When Mrs. Hare started going blind, they closed the school in the middle of the year and moved us all to Wynndel.

It seemed sad and peculiar to me that I couldn't remember the name of this dog. I wanted to hang on to as many memories of Sirdar as I could so on a kind of whim, I began phoning the few people I knew who had also gone to school at Sirdar to ask them what they remembered. They all agreed that Mrs. Hare had a dog but most people disagreed on what it had looked like. Some people thought there were two dogs but no one remembered their names either. It wasn't hard to make the phone calls. There are not many of us and most of us still live in and around the area.

I asked Santo when I saw him in the bar and he said he would ask his sister, who owns the General Store next door, and his cousin who lives up on the hill next door to their grandparents.

I can't remember what Mrs. Hare looked like either, since she always got mixed up in my head with my mother. I have no pictures of the Sirdar school or of Mrs. Hare. We didn't have class pictures. No one I know has any pictures of the school or us or the building that was torn down years ago.

I phoned one more person to ask about the dog. "Yeah, I knew you were going to call," he said. "The dog's name was Terence, he was a black Cocker Spaniel, and he was old, that's why he slept under her desk. Okay?"

But no matter how hard I try, I can't remember Terence, or Mrs. Hare's face, or the sound of her voice, coaxing me through the exciting process of sounding out words as I first learned to read. But I do remember that as soon as I learned to read, I wanted to also write and that Mrs. Hare, of all the people I knew then, didn't seem to think this was a foolish idea.

Chapter Thirteen

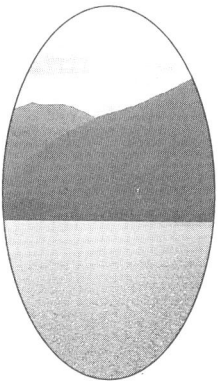

TWO SUMMERS AGO, while I was still living in the city, my son Geronimo phoned and said his ex-partner had agreed to let him have his son for two weeks in August.

"We can meet at the farm," he said. "It will be good for Gaelin to spend some time with his great-grandpa."

I wasn't so sure. Even at eighty, Dad was still a big loud gruff man. Gaelin was nine and, although he had spent time at the farm when he was younger, he had spent most of the last four years in the city. The city was what he was used to.

We stayed in the old farmhouse, which sat empty until I came to visit. Every summer I opened it up, chased out the dust, the spiders, and the ghosts. We settled into our usual summer routine of going to the beach in the afternoon and having dinner with my father in the evenings.

Three years previously, my mother had phoned me at five in the morning. "I fell," she whispered over the phone. "I think I had a stroke." It took me two days to shift my life around and get home and when I did, over my father's objections, I put her in my car and took her to the doctor. The doctor immediately sent to the hospital. I sat beside her bed, watched her belly rise and fall, held her thin hand. She was dehydrated and anemic; she had two broken ribs. My father had somehow not noticed that she had almost stopped eating and drinking. He was terrified of the hospital. As far as he was concerned, it was the place people went to die. But my mother started to recover. Still, it was obvious that she wouldn't be able to come at home and if she did, my father could no longer adequately care for her. My sister and brothers and I talked it over and she was admitted to a care home.

My father had to, finally and reluctantly, learn to look after himself. My mother and I used to find it hilarious that this man, who could fix a broken tractor with haywire, duct tape and a hammer couldn't figure out how to run the washing machine or the microwave. Now that he was forced to cook for himself, his cooking became a kind of freeform invention. He experimented with making soup and jam and even, occasionally, a cake. He canned fruit in the microwave, not worrying when it gave off sparks from the metal lids. He made bread in the bread machine and tomato and carrot juice in the juicer. If he could find a machine to do the cooking for him, then he could manage. He was proud of his new skills and showed them off at length to anyone who would listen.

Nothing at the farm changed except for my mother's absence. My father kept the house exactly the same and, on my visits, I didn't change anything either, except to scrub the fridge and the bathroom. My mother's clothes still hung in the closet, her dressing gown was laid out beside the bed and her notebook lay next to the phone, with long-ago grocery lists still in it. But the place felt vacant. Even when I was a child, I was amazed at how my mother's presence filled the house, how empty it was when she wasn't there, how the house would fill up with energy, warmth, food and comfort the minute she came home.

Chapter Thirteen

We all missed my mother, and we missed her meals. We missed the rich scent of roasting meat and the comfort of collapsing into a chair in front of the TV, knowing we would soon be fed and fed well. In my mother's kitchen we were always children.

Gaelin has always been a fussy eater. Even when he was small, mealtimes were an ordeal; his parents started him off on a vegetarian diet and eventually gave up, resigned to feeding him whatever he would eat. Over the years, he and I have had various grandma/grandson discussions about the problems associated with a diet made up of too much Coke or MacDonald's hamburgers or potato chips. But he was still hard to keep fed. Now, at the farm, every morning I got up early and tried to offer him a decent breakfast, toast and bacon, or porridge, or pancakes with fresh fruit. But still he only nibbled moodily at his food.

At first Gaelin was shy around my father and my father seemed equally shy of him. My father never seemed to be able to remember his name and just referred to him as "the boy." My father was also deaf and he had a habit, when Gaelin said something to him, of staring at him and then ignoring the fact that he had spoken at all. Gaelin never seemed to be sure what to say, or how loudly to say it.

Haying season came. This year it would be my father, my brother, Bill, my son, Geronimo, and my grandson, Gaelin, four generations together. My job was to stay in the house, make sure there was lots to eat and drink, and admire their sunburns, mosquito bites and hay-scratched skin when they came in to take a break.

All day, as they all worked outside, I hovered in the house, in my mother's kitchen, among my mother's pots and pans and familiar things. It felt like my mother would bustle in at any moment, putting the kettle on for tea, tidying, setting things to right, making the house feel warm, comfortable, a home again. Now I tried to take her place—I made a pot of chicken soup and my mother's special cheese biscuits for lunch, I made lemonade and gingersnaps and, while I cooked and tidied and washed the dishes, I couldn't help staring out the window at the distant hay field, listening to the roar of the tractor and wondering how Gaelin was faring. I missed my mother with an intensity that only increased as the day went on. It seemed so unfair, so wrong, that she wasn't here.

The men folk trooped in for lunch, talking of tractors and weather, how much was done and how much was left to do. Gaelin seemed quiet. I asked him how his morning went; it turned out he had spent the morning sitting beside his great-grandfather on the tractor, had taken a turn at driving this ancient rusting machine which my father had continued to patch together from parts of other machines for all the years we have been on the farm.

After lunch I asked Gaelin if he wouldn't rather stay in with me, or go to the beach, or help me make cookies. He looked at me. "No," he said, "We've got to get the hay in." I fussed at him about wearing a hat and sunscreen and he ignored me and went back out with his great-grandpa, his great-uncle, and his father.

By the end of the day, I could tell he was exhausted and sunburnt. I finally prevailed and took him off to the beach for a swim. When we came back up from the beach, we ate homegrown beef and new potatoes from the garden for supper and, for dessert, there was ice cream and strawberries. Gaelin hadn't eaten much of the main course and now he loaded his bowl with ice cream and the lion's share of the strawberries.

"Gaelin," I said, "that's too much. Leave some for others."

"Let the kid have what he wants, " growled my father. I stared while he took Gaelin's bowl and loaded it with the remaining strawberries. Gaelin shot me a triumphant look and ate the whole thing. After supper we all fell into bed early, knowing there was still another couple of days of hard work ahead.

In the morning I woke, listening for the early morning sounds I love, the swallows under the eaves, the chickens in the yard and the

Chapter Thirteen

breeze in the giant cedar trees. Gaelin was almost always awake first; he would get up by himself and play quietly or draw pictures until I got up. But this morning he was nowhere around. I trotted across the yard to my father's house, came in the door, and there was Gaelin, sitting with my dad, eating breakfast.

"Hey," said my father, "this kid's got better sense than you. He likes my cooking."

Gaelin was sitting beside my father, eating the bread my father had made, covered with runny black currant jam. He had a full glass of my father's tomato juice in front of him.

All my life, my father has been trying to make me drink tomato juice and all my life I have detested it. My fussy grandson picked up his glass, drained it and held it out to his great-grandpa to be refilled.

I had a piece of toast and a cup of my father's weak grey coffee. We talked about the hay, the weather, and when we would all have a chance to go visit my mother.

And then I went and sat on the porch and watched my father and his great-grandson walk side by side down the driveway to where the ancient tractor waited for them under the cedar trees.

When I was a child, everything around me was wild, or I thought it was and I thought I could be wild as well. It seemed to be right, to be wild, not part of the confusing world of houses and people and rules that made little sense. Town and people were far away—we had neighbours, but even they were wild, or seemed wild to me, and all things wild and free seemed to me where I belonged as well.

Now I look at mountains that are torn and seamed with roads, scabbed with slowly healing clear cuts, and I know the wild is still there, still underneath waiting, just as it waits in cities and under pavement and highways and high-rises, behind dams, power lines, oil and gas pipelines, behind and between and under metal and glass and concrete.

My life was acted out against this landscape that even when it is altered, remains fundamentally unchanged. The place and I have grown into each other. I am now this place where I live, weathered, seamed, covered with the traces of everything that has happened to me but, fundamentally, the same person who fell into belonging when I was five.

I live at the farm now. My father died of cancer and my brother Bill and I decided we would do whatever we could to fight off the tourists, the tax-collectors and the real-estate dealers to keep the farm intact. He is replanting the orchard and re-building the fences and I potter in the garden and take the dogs for walks.

I stayed in Vancouver for seven years, living in a landscape of cars and buildings and noise and exhaust fumes. When I left, it seemed odd to me that I had lived somewhere for so long and still couldn't find anything about it to love. I loved so much of what I did there: classes at the university, playing with my grandson at the park on Sunday afternoons, going for coffee with friends at the small crowded coffee shop down the street, movies, sushi with the family on Friday nights. But I couldn't love the city itself nor could I find any place in it to which I could feel connected.

My life there was bounded by the university, by the library, by my grown children—who all lived nearby—and my grandchildren. And then one night, when I was almost finished both this book and my last degree, I had a dream that the university was next to the mountains at the farm. In the dream, I realized I could walk away from the university and into the trees anytime I wanted or needed to.

When I woke, I realized that the split in my life, between books and the farm, between the forest and poetry, had somehow eased, if not completely healed.

Now that I am home again, I spend a part of every day breathing in the silence. All my life I have sunk my dreams, hopes and fears into this one place, asked it to carry them. Now I have planted my

Chapter Thirteen

future in the garden, under the marigolds and sunflowers, willing for the earth to hold me there, keep me safe.

One November night, when I was finally home from the city, I walked back in the dark from the lake. The moon was coming up behind the Purcells, behind a black and white slanted slab of hill. The light framed my shadow. I stood still and the wind blew spiny bits of snow at me. All I could do was breathe and breathe.

All I wanted was to be here walking in the cold night, the moon rising over the mountains and the light falling over the farm where, just at the edge of the field, the coyotes were taunting the dogs, the coyotes in their snowy woods beyond the fence and the dogs running in the pasture, while the sleepy, grumpy cows shook their heads at the dogs, and I went on standing in the cold instead of going inside.

The Colours of the Columbia Series by Maa Press aims to celebrate and give voice to the people and land of the Columbia Basin and the Columbia Mountains of Western North America through radically and reliably regional books. Get to know the region by collecting them all! Visit www.maapress.ca to view the Colours of the Columbia titles. As of 2007, the series contains the following:

Green Book – *The Inner Green: Exploring Home in the Columbia Mountains*, by K.Linda Kivi and Eileen Delehanty Pearkes, 2005.

Gold Book – *The Purcell Suite: Upholding the Wild*, edited by K.Linda Kivi and co-published with Wildsight, 2007.

Blue Book – *Blue Valley: An Ecological Memoir*, by Luanne Armstrong, 2007.